AN ALTERNATE PRAGMATISM
FOR GOING PUBLIC

T0325244

AN ALTERNATE PRAGMATISM FOR GOING PUBLIC

Jim Webber

UTAH STATE UNIVERSITY PRESS
Logan

© 2018 by the University Press of Colorado

Published by Utah State University Press
An imprint of University Press of Colorado
5589 Arapahoe Avenue, Suite 206C
Boulder, Colorado 80303

ASSOCIATION
of UNIVERSITY
PRESSES

The University Press of Colorado is a proud member
of the Association of University Presses.

The University Press of Colorado is a cooperative publishing enterprise sup-
ported, in part, by Adams State College, Colorado State University, Fort Lewis
College, Metropolitan State College of Denver, Regis University, University
of Colorado, University of Northern Colorado, Utah State University, and
Western State College of Colorado.

∞ This paper meets the requirements of the ANSI/NISO Z39.48-1992
    (Permanence of Paper).

ISBN: 978-1-60732-653-3 (paper)
ISBN: 978-1-60732-654-0 (e-book)
DOI: https://doi.org/10.7330/9781607326540

Library of Congress Cataloging-in-Publication Data

Names: Webber, James (Professor), author.
Title: An alternate pragmatism for going public / James Webber.
Description: Logan : Utah State University Press, [2017] | Includes biblio-
    graphical references and index.
Identifiers: LCCN 2017007054| ISBN 9781607326533 (pbk.) | ISBN
    9781607326540 (ebook)
Subjects: LCSH: English language—Rhetoric—Study and teaching (Higher) |
    Pragmatism. | Educational change—United States. | Education and state—
    United States.
Classification: LCC PE1404 .W426 2017 | DDC 808/.0420711—dc23
LC record available at https://lccn.loc.gov/2017007054

Cover image © Iurii Kiliian/Shutterstock.com

CONTENTS

ACKNOWLEDGMENTS

Donald Graves (1985) argues that all children can write, pro-vided they have four things: choice of topic, time to write, responses to their writing, and the opportunity to form a com-munity of learners. I have found my needs to be remarkably similar while writing this book.

While I was a graduate student at the University of New Hampshire, Tom Newkirk, Christina Ortmeier-Hooper, Christy Beemer, Paula Salvio, and Larry Prelli helped me take a first pass at the topic of this book, although I didn't yet have terms for it. Subsequent conversations with my friend Maja Wilson helped me discover that I was trying to write about composi-tion's rhetoric of professionalism.

At the University of Nevada, Reno, colleagues Cathy Chaput, Justin Gifford, Lynda Walsh, Melissa Nicolas, and David Rondel helped me build on this discovery. Ashley Marshall, James Mardock, Bill Macauley, Elizabeth Francis, and Kathy Boardman then encouraged me through more drafts. Meanwhile, conver-sations with PhD students in Rhetoric and Composition sug-gested new angles on the political economy of educational expertise. Katie Miller, Merrilyne Lundahl, Phil Goodwin, and Austin Kelly have been and continue to be fellow travelers.

All this time, I relied on two writing groups. Since 2008, the Boston Group has been reading my dead ends. Thanks go to Gesa Kirsch, Patty Wilde, Erin Wecker, and Rose Keefe for their generosity and patience! Starting in 2012, the Reno Writing Group of Katherine Fusco, Mikaela Rogozen-Soltar, and Amy Pason also kindly read some early drafts of chapters.

Conversations with colleagues in the field also helped me en-vision audiences for this book. At multiple meetings of the Con-ference on College Composition and Communication (CCCC) and the Rhetoric Society of America (RSA), Amy Wan, Scott Wible, Chris Gallagher, and Robert Asen suggested new ways I could explore the relationships among rhetoric, composition, and public policy. Likewise, when an earlier version of chapter 3 was under review at *College Composition and Communication* (*CCC*), editor Jonathan Alexander and the anonymous *CCC* reviewers helped me situate my argument more clearly within composition studies, and the revision of the article later allowed me to re-envision the overall arc of the book.

Speaking of this arc: I am grateful for the opportunity to re-envision it. Utah State University Press Editor Michael Spooner offered the encouragements and challenges I needed to discover a more interesting and nuanced argument than the one I'd set out to make. The anonymous reviewers of USUP likewise prompted me to attempt a more generous form of engagement with our field(s).

Throughout this process, my family cheered me on. Thanks and love always go to my parents, Jan and Phil Webber, and to my siblings Sylvia, Hanneli, and Mark.

Last but not least, I am grateful to my dearest Catrina, who never chided me for saying "I had a breakthrough!" every day for months when my revision of this book had finally picked up steam. I can't wait to share more of what's next.

Parts of chapter 3 were published as "Toward an Artful Critique of Reform: Responding to Standards, Assessment, and Machine Scoring" in the September 2017 issue of *CCC* (69.1: 118–45). Permission to reprint granted by the National Council of Teachers of English.

AN ALTERNATE PRAGMATISM
FOR GOING PUBLIC

INTRODUCTION

Pragmatism figures prominently in multiple lines of composition inquiry. Scholars invoke the term, the value, and the philosophical tradition to ground professional judgment in pedagogy (Durst 1999; Roskelly and Ronald 1998; Spellmeyer 1993), writing program administration (Adler-Kassner 2008; R. Miller 1998a; Porter et al. 2000; Strickland 2011), assessment (Adler-Kassner and O'Neill 2010; Gallagher 2012), and community engagement (Flower 2008; Long 2008). While these scholars address divergent concerns and often advance contending perspectives, their invocations of pragmatism reflect a common concern. Each scholar seeks to articulate a rhetorical wisdom *inside* the profession for advancing our values *outside* the profession. And, each forwards this wisdom in hope of formulating a shared standard of judgment for "going public" (Mortensen 1998). Such a standard would not impose a single approach for all teachers, scholars, and administrators in every context, but it would offer a standpoint broadly shared enough to enable cooperative inquiry and action in composition.

Articulating such a wisdom is a tall order. We go public to assert our professional standing, as when we issue position statements on institution-, system-, and national-level policies. But we also go public to sponsor inquiry among "ordinary people" (Long 2008, 14), like students, parents, and community members, in the hope of shaping institutional, political, and public discussions of literacy education. These aims are not mutually exclusive, but they do tend to pull us in different directions. (Re)asserting our standing seeks to maintain the rhetorical and sociological boundaries of professionalism: we want policy to reflect *our* terms for *our* values. Sponsoring inquiry may share this aim, but it also seeks to broaden public participation in

DOI: 10.7330/9781607326540.c000

debates over shared concerns: we want to help our publics *discover* terms adequate to *their* experiences with literacy. When we invoke pragmatism in composition, we attempt to reconcile these aims. We give a name to a set of contingent judgments about professionalism, publics, rhetoric, and experience. Pragmatism is our word for the possibility of a public rhetoric of professionalism—and for the possibility of a shared standard of wisdom that can ground the use of this rhetoric.

Pragmatism is also a fighting word. This assertion may sound dubious when we frequently celebrate pragmatic judgment in our teaching, research, and administration. But our claims of pragmatism start fights because we use them not only to praise but also to discipline fellow professionals' judgment for going public. For instance, pragmatism names the reason we must do more than publicly critique problematic institutional policies or political reforms: such a response is unlikely to secure policy outcomes now and may offer us little opportunity to reappropriate or redirect these policies later. This appeal assures us that if we'd account for the constraints of our various contexts, both those presently evident and those likely to appear in the future, we'd wisely adopt an alternate means of going public.

Responses to this claim, however, reject its standard of rhetorical wisdom. A pragmatism of reappropriation and redirection, critics argue, tends to limit professionals to the discourses advanced by institutional and political reforms. In the contemporary moment, for example, we may claim that *we* best deliver globally competitive graduates because our judgment is expert and consistent, but such a response risks reducing us to service providers vying for market share within the neoliberal order of reform. In this view, redirection may, for the time being, preserve some functions of professional standing, but in the long run, such a tactic is likely to concede professionalism to the competing social logics of bureaucracy and markets.[1] Moreover, such a tactic risks collapsing the democratic aims of professionalism under the rubric of management-for-competition. These potential consequences suggest an alternate standard of rhetorical judgment: if we oppose reform, we should say what we mean, in our terms.

This standoff turns on competing claims of wisdom: there is or isn't room for critique to reopen debate; redirecting reform can or can't advance our values. Debate over these claims, however, is ongoing and commonplace in composition. What makes these claims truly contentious is their *style*. Each claim tends to elevate its contestable political judgments to the status of realism. That is, if you critique (or reappropriate or redirect) reform, you fail to understand the political economy of reform, and if you don't understand *that*, you can't serve the public goods of composition. As members of a profession, we need a shared standard of rhetorical judgment, and for such a standard to be shared, there must be discipline. *This* is what makes pragmatism a fighting word.

Given these stakes, it might seem more productive to set aside pragmatism as composition's key term for going public. But my argument is that despite its agonistic freight, pragmatism can be worth the trouble. When we invoke pragmatism, we envision a wisdom adequate for re-linking professional and public goods amid the neoliberal energy of reform. Even when we acknowledge that our claims to such wisdom are partial and contingent, the promise of improved professional judgment draws us back into a collective process of inquiry and innovation. In our local contexts, we resolve to reassess the adequacy of our rhetorical means to the professional and democratic ends of going public. And in our disciplinary conversations, we recommit to circulating, reassessing, and extending these local inquiries. Pragmatism goads us to move discussion from inquiry to theory to action and back to inquiry again.

As the opening paragraphs suggest, however, this discussion tends toward stalemate. While composition's debate runs deeper than style, our inquiry into going public appears to begin and end with our claims to pragmatism. To reopen our conversation, I argue, we need to develop an alternate rhetorical style, one that can recuperate and extend pragmatism's potential for inquiry. In making this argument, I am agreeing *in part* with philosopher Ruth Anna Putnam's (1998, 63) lament that "pragmatism means too many things to too many people."

The capaciousness of the term can both invite and hinder collaborative inquiry, but this book does not attempt to declare a "correct" pragmatism for going public. Instead, it highlights what we tend to minimize in our most prominent rhetorical enactments of pragmatism. My hope with this recovery and reinscription is that an alternate perspective on our rhetorical judgment can reopen and extend inquiry into going public.

To pursue this aim, I read composition's critique/redirection debate as an "adjacent" critic. As philosopher Colin Koopman (2009, 39) describes this positioning, such a critic is "not quite apart from the social practices they criticize and yet also not quite wholly inside of them either." Rather than entering our debate as it is currently framed, then, I seek to reorient it. I explore how arguments for critique and redirection invoke pragmatism as a resource for defending professionalism against the competing social logics of bureaucracy and markets. But I argue that this approach crops out an equally important dimension of the pragmatic tradition, what I call its antiprofessionalism, or its capacity to reopen public debates, like those over reform, to the participation of those outside professional spheres. I draw out the antiprofessionalism of the pragmatic tradition to envision an alternate response to reform, not as a replacement to our existing innovations, but as a complementary approach we are likely to need in the future. An alternate pragmatism for going public, I argue, commits us not to redirecting reform or reasserting professionalism but to sponsoring dissenting public participation as a potential means of authorizing our professional judgment.

Such antiprofessionalism is admittedly risky in the contemporary neoliberal moment. Critical public participation may affirm our judgment, or it may embrace consumer choice in a competitive marketplace of service providers. Innovating on our defenses of professionalism, then, could actually undermine our standing to define the goals and measures of public education in literacy. But as I argue in the following chapters, the pragmatic tradition envisions the enlargement of public participation as more than a threat to professionals. A broader role for such participation in policy debate can also create more opportunities for our publics to authorize composition professionals' judgment as a public good. This is the central wager of this book: that a rhetoric of publicness can help us accomplish what our rhetoric of professionalism has not. But what we accomplish via an alternate pragmatism is unlikely to match what we have conventionally envisioned as the aim of going public. Rather than defending our professional standing, we may end up transforming it. An alternate pragmatism seeks to reconcile critical public participation and professional expertise at a time when contemporary reforms work to separate them.

I don't believe such a transformation would be a bad thing. It would respond to the neoliberal political economy of reform and to the democratic commitments of the philosophically pragmatic tradition. But such a transformation is deeply contingent, so this book focuses more on elaborating an alternate rhetorical style for inquiry within composition than on codifying strategies for public action. My primary resource for this style is what communication rhetorician Paul Stob (2016) terms pragmatism's oscillation between "tender-" and "tough-mindedness." This pivot suggests a way to appreciate, qualify, and potentially extend the work of teachers, scholars, and administrators engaged in composition's conversation about going public. Too much tender-mindedness may envision a seemingly boundless capacity for democratic public participation to authorize professional judgment. Too much tough-mindedness may envision little or none. Pragmatism's stylistic turn allows for a kind of critical hope in the way that we talk to each other about the work of going public amid the crush of reform. Building more broadly shared grounds for this hope is my aim with this book.

Still, as Kenneth Burke (1969a, 357) reminds us, "constitutions are agonistic instruments," so while this book aims to further cooperative inquiry within composition, it also sets a course for a certain kind of inquiry. My terms for chiding are discipline, narrowing, and conventionality. My terms for enthusiasm are dissent, public, and potential. As terminological oppositions go, these are pretty conventional. But what this book hopes to offer is new reasons for these terms. Rather than advancing dissent as politically preferential to management, I forward antiprofessionalism as an alternate pragmatic innovation on going public. When we invoke pragmatism for responding to reform, I argue, such invocations should encompass wisdom not only for pursuing institutional and professional consequences but also for attending to the broader democratic consequences of our rhetoric.

Finally, about the terms of this book. I forward a map of composition's conversations about going public, grouping our innovations under the headings of bureaucracy, reframing, and public engagement. I call professionals' reappropriation of appeals to standardization a bureaucratic innovation because this tactic borrows the rhetorical strategy favored by the social logic of bureaucracy: promising the efficient delivery of skills through standardization. That being said, the scholars and critics whose perspectives I discuss under the rubric of bureaucracy are varied and often in disagreement. What unites these scholars and critics is not so much their political commitments as their rhetorical willingness to repurpose appeals to standardization for professional aims. I am not arguing that this willingness in itself is mistaken. Rather, I am arguing that this willingness deserves critical assessment in light of its potential consequences for our publics' participation in reform.

Similarly, I recognize reframing as the willingness to redirect neoliberal reforms' appeals to a competitive world. The tactic of redirection aims to expand contemporary reforms like the Common Core when professional critiques appear to have had little effect. Again, as with the term bureaucracy, the scholars associated with reframing forward a range of perspectives on going public. What is shared, however, is a judgment about rhetorical style—a readiness to expand composition's rhetoric of professionalism to encompass reform's appeals to competition. I am not arguing that this readiness in itself is unwise, but I do trace out the potential consequences of this rhetorical expansion for engaging the full range of composition's publics.

Finally, I term the reassertion of our professionalism as a public good "public engagement" because the central concern is broadening participation in authorizing professional judgment. As above, the scholars I associate with public engagement are diverse, but their rhetorical style tends to center on the key appeal of professionalism, the democratic representation afforded by our expert judgment in context. While this appeal is longstanding in composition, I explore what are perhaps the unintended public consequences of professionals' reliance on this appeal amid contemporary reform.

In naming these innovations on going public, my intention is to call attention to their rhetorical enactments of pragmatic aims. The purpose of this taxonomy is *not* to suggest a qualitative progression from the problematic to the praiseworthy. In other words, I am not presenting composition's innovations on going public with the intention of arriving at my own perspective as the culmination of pragmatic inquiry. If such a progressive taxonomy presents innovation in a straight line, my taxonomy might be visualized as a bicycle wheel. Spokes radiate outward from a hub. Pragmatism is the hub, the goad and resource of innovation. Bureaucracy, reframing, and public engagement turn inward toward the hub and then turn outward, overlapping as spokes do. These overlaps indicate that no one approach is terribly different from another in origin; moreover, each approach remains connected to the others as discussion and action progress. But the innovations of bureaucracy, reframing, and public engagement do radiate outward, and so they do tend toward decreasing commensurability. My effort here is to put these pragmatic innovations into conversation with each other when their rhetorical styles tend to prevent such conversation. Based on this conversation, I believe, we can think anew about possible forms of action for contending with current and future K–16 reforms.

NOTE

1. As I discuss further in this chapter, I read professionalism as "the third logic" (Freidson 2001). Against the standardization of bureaucracy, professionalism maintains an emphasis on expert judgment in context. Against the consumer choice promoted by markets, professionalism

asserts the standing of experts to make judgment on behalf of the public good. This is the central struggle of "going public" in composition—to defend our professionalism against the bureaucratic standardization and market competition promoted by contemporary K–16 reforms.

Chapter 1

"IS STRATEGIC INSTRUMENTALISM THE BEST WE CAN DO?"

During a recent Conference on College Composition and Communication (CCCC) presentation, I summarized the central appeal of contemporary K–16 articulation reforms: in the globally competitive present, only common standards and assessments can improve *all* students' access to opportunity. From this perspective, writing teachers', scholars', and administrators' rejection of standardization should not be understood as a public defense of professional judgment. Rather, this rejection should be understood as an admission of failure to recognize the way the world is. Such a failure requires transformative change, for when composition expertise no longer serves the public good, professionals can no longer deserve their privileged standing to define the goals and measures of public education in literacy. A competitive world requires a competitive marketplace of expertise, for only good markets can make for good democracy.

This appeal is rarely stated *quite* so flatly. The Common Core claims that increasing students' access to college and careers requires internationally benchmarked standards and assessments. Likewise, Complete College America insists that underprepared students can "complete to compete" only when "remediation" (basic writing) has been eliminated. And the Collegiate Learning Assessment (CLA) maintains that standardized outcomes assessments alone can ensure that college graduates are adequately prepared for the global workplace. But the political-economic stakes of these reform proposals are

DOI: 10.7330/9781607326540.c001

clear. Since policies based in professional judgment offer poor returns on investment, educational expertise itself must become competitive. Only *then* can expertise serve democracy. I argued that the success of this appeal, demonstrated by corporate-political platforms becoming policy at the institution and state levels, suggests that we in composition need to reconsider how *access* works in public debate. What was once "our" term is now part of the lexicon of reform, and our conventional appeal, that professional judgment in context ensures the democratic representation of our diverse publics, is being displaced by another vision, in which increasing access requires a policy marketplace that invites public choice among competing providers of expertise.[1] In such a marketplace, it doesn't matter whether professionals or testing companies and political think thanks define the goals and measures of public education in literacy; it only matters who can codify the skills students need for success in the globally competitive scene. If choice among service providers displaces teachers', scholars', and administrators' professional standing, that is simply democratic participation in action.

In discussion after the panel, an audience member asked a question tinged with resignation: "is strategic instrumentalism the best we can do?" In other words, if the link between democratic ends and professional judgment is being eroded, must we abandon our conventional appeals to pluralism and counter reform's claims of skills and results with the promise of more skills and better results? Rather than reappropriating the discourse of reform, I suggested, we might begin to counter groups like Complete College America (CCA) by renewing composition's longstanding efforts to represent basic writers' experiences (Adler-Kassner and Harrington 2002; Horner and Lu 1999; Lu 1992; Rose 1985; Rose 1988). Inviting our publics' inquiry into current students' experiences, I argued, could foster alternatives to CCA's images of basic writing as waste and futility. Moreover, such images could dramatize "access" in ways that our conventional appeal to professionalism as the bulwark of democracy might not. But I couldn't say more at the time about how we might innovate on going public amid the constraints of contemporary K–16 reform.

Since that discussion, I have attempted to unravel the thicket of issues implied in the audience member's question, and this book is the result of that inquiry. If our rhetoric of professionalism is being displaced by the rhetoric of standardization-for-competition-for-democracy, how should we innovate on the ways we go public? Specifically, as the audience member wondered, should we reappropriate and redirect the rhetoric(s) of reform in the hope of steering the development of corporate-political standards and assessments? Or, as the weary tone of the audience member suggested, should we reassert our professional judgment in our preferred terms despite the limits of our appeals in the contemporary scene? Or should we envision an alternate rhetoric of professionalism?

In the following chapters, I explore and engage with scholars' responses to these questions. Following Joseph Harris (2012), my aim is a "sympathetic counterstatement" (xi) to the disciplinary conversation about going public. I recognize the redirection of reform and the reassertion of professionalism as composition's primary rhetorical means of advancing our pluralistic judgment, and I appreciate these strategies as nuanced negotiations amid profound constraints. But I also explore how these strategies can limit our pursuit of an equally important aim, building professionals' potential to foster democratic public participation in reform. I trace this limit to pragmatism, the value that scholars frequently invoke to guide their innovations on going public. For example, pragmatism authorizes scholars' calls to reappropriate the discourses of institutional standardization (e.g., R. Miller 1998a) and redirect neoliberal reforms as a means of advancing composition's democratic aims (e.g., Adler-Kassner 2008; Adler-Kassner and Harrington 2010; Adler-Kassner and O'Neill 2010; Fleckenstein 2008). These scholars open critical inquiry into the consequences of going public and call for an alternate response to the political economy of reform. And, as I explore in the following chapters, such responses can claim demonstrable policy outcomes. However, I argue that these pragmatic innovations can also minimize our attention to the public consequences of reappropriating and redirecting reform discourses that construe democratic participation as assent to management or consumer choice.

I identify a similar selection and deflection of attention in the reassertion of professionalism. Scholars emphasize the need for our contextual inquiry into diverse contexts of literacy teaching, learning, and assessment to inform education policy (e.g., Gallagher 2011). Since we perform this inquiry, the policy implication of "being there" is clear: only *our* professional judgment can be counted on to serve the public good. Here, pragmatism authorizes us to claim our professional inquiry as a form of public representation. This claim rightly reasserts our epistemic advantage over the acontextual standardization-for-competition of neoliberal reform. But this pragmatic innovation, I argue, can also minimize our attention to the democratic consequences of our claim to possess an expertise that we alone can exercise in the name of the public.

My concern with these pragmatic innovations is that while they attend to the professional consequences of going public, they also limit our attention to the public consequences of our rhetorical judgment. This is not to say that public goods are unimportant to the scholars cited above; indeed, the stated aims of bureaucracy, reframing, and public engagement are to increase students' democratic access to opportunity. Rather, I am arguing that these pragmatic innovations are working from limited rhetorical resources. These resources are the primary rhetorics of reform: namely, appeals to bureaucratic standardization, market competition, and professionalism. These appeals tend to minimize roles for our publics in debate over how to improve K–16 literacy teaching, learning, and assessment.[2] Instead, these rhetorics construe public voice as a choice among predetermined, politically secured options in the political economy: governmental standardization for the sake of efficiency, market choice for the sake of competition, or professional judgment for the sake of public representation. Minimized in such a choice, however, is a role for our publics in assessing and potentially authorizing our contextual judgment as responsiveness to public experience with writing. To foster such public participation in reform, I argue, entails expanding composition's efforts at redirecting reform or reasserting professionalism. Rather than defending our professionalism by narrowing the role of public participation in reform, an alternate response would seek to enlarge it.

To pursue this aim, I recover an alternate pragmatism for going public. I explore composition's innovations genealogically by reading the pragmatism invoked against the pragmatism enacted. Like contemporary proposals to reappropriate the rhetoric of bureaucracy (e.g., Graff and Birkenstein 2008), I heed William James's (1907) call to attend to consequences. I recognize the need for a rhetoric of professionalism that can secure material benefits for all students amid the neoliberal energy of contemporary reform. But in addition to recognizing the material consequences of going public, I call equal attention to the experiential consequences of our rhetoric—how it might form non-expert publics around the questions of reform. Based on this broadened conception of consequences, I reimagine pragmatism not only as a warrant for professionals to reappropriate the discourse of standardization but also as a prompt to renew our inquiry into public experiences with literacy, experiences that can qualify reform's calls to eliminate "remediation." Like proposals to redirect the market-driven rhetoric of contemporary reform (e.g., Adler-Kassner 2008), I find common cause with Cornel West's (1989) "prophetic pragmatism": I recognize the need for professionals to do more than denounce reform. But my reading of West suggests not only the limits but also the potential of professional critiques to sponsor public participation in discussions of key reform proposals like machine scoring. And, like proposals to reassert professional judgment (e.g., Gallagher 2011), I draw on John Dewey's (1927) vision of public professionalism. I recognize the need for our local judgment to scale up to the political economy of reform. But in addition to claiming our privileged standing to make judgments on behalf of our publics, I also envision a rhetorical means of sponsoring critical public participation that can authorize our contextual judgment (and not externally-imposed outcomes assessments) as responsiveness to public experiences with literacy.

The aim of this recovery and reinscription of pragmatism is to forward a goad and resource for composition's efforts at going public. An alternate pragmatism prompts us to tell a different story about our professionalism, one that resists the tendency of reform debate to reduce our judgment to the conventional political-economic grounds of standardization, competition, or expertise. But while such a story disrupts our conventions of going public, it also offers us a resource for innovation focused on our unique potential in contemporary reform debate. Unlike bureaucratic standardization and market competition as models for public policy, an alternate pragmatism recognizes composition professionals' capacity to foster critical public participation in national discussions about the teaching, learning, and assessment of writing. The point of sponsoring this participation is not only to promote our contextual judgment as superior to the standardization forwarded by proponents of bureaucracy or markets, although I imagine few professionals would object to that aim. Rather, the larger goal of sponsoring engagement is to enable our local publics to assess the adequacy of contemporary standardization-for-competition to reflect their experiences with writing. The hope of such engagement is that it can reshape broader public discussions of reform when we scale up, or circulate accounts of the local, the contextual, and the participatory to sponsor similar inquiries in other contexts. The story of an alternate rhetoric of professionalism, in other words, is one of local engagement as a driver of national engagement. With national discussions of reform stalemated between calls for market competition and professionalism, I read fostering critical public participation as a potential third way for us in composition to go public.

SCALING DOWN TO SCALE UP

This rhetorical engagement with the political economy of reform is an attempt to scale up from local experience. Starting in 2010, Maja Wilson and I interviewed middle school parents about their children's writing in language arts classes (Webber and Wilson 2012, Webber and Wilson 2013). We wanted to know how parents assessed a local teacher's progressive pedagogy against the backdrop of national attention to the then-emerging Common Core. More broadly, we wondered if professionalism's characteristic appeals to pluralistic contextualism could contend with national reforms' appeals to standardization-for-competition-for-equity. To our surprise, professional contextualism fared better than expected, but only when parents approached it through a process of inquiry. For example, in one conversation with parents, we learned about an eighth-grade boy's attempt to emulate the writing of the Beats. This writing unnerved the boy's parents since it resisted conventional expectations of propriety and tone, and these parents accused their son's teacher of not "doing her job" by allowing space for stylistic experimentation instead of exclusively emphasizing conventional correctness. But as these parents talked more, they admitted that their son's pursuit of facility in a style helped him use school assignments for his own purposes. And this shift in orientation, the parents acknowledged, helped their son see writing as an activity in which he could invest himself deeply. By the end of the conversation, these parents' inquiry into their son's act of writing helped them re-envision writing as more than the mastery of conventional styles and professional judgment as more than common standards.

We took from this study the insight that "public values are more capacious than public discourse" about literacy education (Webber and Wilson 2013, 217). And, we took from this conversation a methodological orientation for public engagement resembling what Jeffrey Grabill (2012) calls a "research stance." That is, we formed "a set of beliefs and obligations" (211) that shaped how we acted as researchers. We recognized that local inquiry into acts of teaching, learning, and assessment could, in admittedly limited ways, open space for discussion beyond the logic of standardization-for-competition. Based on this insight, I began to wonder whether composition professionals could invite similar public inquiry into the acts of writing central to *college* reforms. Could we in composition prompt our students to evaluate the proposals of groups like Complete College America and the Collegiate Learning Assessment as responses to their experiences with writing? And could we circulate accounts of such local inquiry to sponsor critical public discussions of nationally prominent K–16 reforms? Could we scale up in a different way?

These questions arose at a time when it was hard *not* to foresee corporate-political groups displacing composition professionals' standing to define the goals and measures of public education in literacy. As recently as 2012, the Common Core and its assessments were being implemented in forty-three states (Common Core State Standards Initiative 2015), and over seven hundred institutions in the United States and abroad had adopted the CLA to "benchmark value-added growth in student learning" (Council for Aid to Education 2016). In 2017, however, the trajectory of these reforms appears less certain. At the K–12 level, the Opt Out movement has publicly, if incrementally, undermined implementation of Core-aligned assessments (Saultz and Evans 2015; Strauss 2016). At the college level, the Voluntary System of Accountability (2012) now recognizes the American Association of Colleges and Universities' (AAC&U) VALUE rubrics for reporting learning outcomes, suggesting that, at least for the time being, the goals and measures of college writing are to be defined by faculty in specific contexts rather than by groups like the CLA.[3]

Still, the lifecycles of past K–16 reforms suggest that neoliberal standardization often succeeds by "failing." Even though the American Diploma Project never went national with its college- and career-readiness measures in the early-to-mid-2000s, it cultivated the "state-based" strategy that moved the Common Core from corporate-political platform to public policy reality.[4] Despite the recent slowing of the Common Core, this strategy continues with CCA's efforts to measure "pre-major learning," particularly students' writing development in introductory-level courses (Complete College America 2011). CCA seeks data to determine whether public institutions are moving students quickly toward majors, programs, and credentials. The ultimate goal of CCA is a system of "performance funding," a policy lever for governors to incentivize greater efficiency in instruction (Complete College America 2013). Only greater efficiency, CCA argues, can strengthen state economies and students' preparation for the global marketplace, and only public choice among increasingly efficient options can transform higher education to serve its democratizing function.

The political horizon of performance funding reminds us that even if the Common Core and the CLA are slowing in the face of public and professional recalcitrance, we in composition are likely to face these reforms' appeals again soon. We may be able to redirect CLA-style reforms within our professional spheres as the AAC&U has done. But we may also need to contend with these reforms in public debate, and in this work we are likely to struggle. Groups like CCA successfully exploit the commonsense of college students and parents as consumers rather than as partners of writing teachers, scholars, and administrators. Within this market frame of reform, neoliberal standardization is *the* public good: common outcomes allow states to measure public institutions' performance, performance data allows public choice among institutions, and public choice drives innovation in efficiency. We in composition have recognized this choice-for-efficiency as a means of displacing our professional judgment, and in our scholarly journals and professional associations, we have decried the Common Core's tendency toward formalism (Bomer et al. 2009; Hansen 2012; Summerfield and Anderson 2012;) the K–12 assessment consortia's reliance on machine scoring (Anson et al. 2013), and the Collegiate Learning Assessment's methodology (Haswell 2012). We have forwarded these critiques to demonstrate our professional judgment and to argue that reformers cannot serve the writing needs and experiences of our diverse publics. Yet our critical responses to reform's "innovation" have not invited the public participation that appears to be blunting K–12 reformers' calls for neoliberal standardization.

Given the likely public contests to come, we will need to innovate on the ways we go public. But how? This question arises at another moment of transition. The last few years saw college student action on issues ranging from athletics to race to sexual violence.[5] These actions frequently concerned inquiry into administrative decisions made on students' behalf. In one of the most prominent cases, the University of Missouri group Concerned Student 1950 publicized campus leaders' efforts to address racial equality. Concerned 1950 issued a list of demands, such as removing Missouri System President Tim Wolfe, increasing black faculty and staff system-wide, and developing a strategic plan for increasing minority student retention.[6] After displays of solidarity with Concerned 1950, in which faculty threatened a campus-wide walkout and the Missouri football team refused to play, President Wolfe resigned. These events were notable in Missouri to be sure, but this critical action scaled up beyond the local when accounts of mass student demonstration circulated online and sponsored similar events at other institutions. In the terms of publics theory, students at Missouri and elsewhere assembled critical counterpublics around their concerns and successfully demanded policy change.[7]

Like the publics of composition amid reform, the publics of student action are both local and national. But unlike the largely professional publics envisioned in composition's responses to reform, student actions like those in Missouri sought to sponsor counterpublic resistance as a response to power. That is, student action recognized the potential for otherwise marginalized and excluded publics to participate in debate about higher education policy. These actions' tenor was one of antiprofessionalism—experientially grounded resistance to rhetorics of power in higher education—and in 2015, this antiprofessionalism appeared more powerful than our appeals to professionalism amid reform. When following the student actions of 2015–16, I was struck by the potential common ground between the antiprofessionalism of college protests and that of the K–12 parents Maja Wilson and I interviewed. In both cases, local inquiry demonstrated the potential to unsettle seemingly impervious rhetorics of power in public discussions of education. And while this inquiry was local in our experience with parents, it scaled up in the student case. It circulated its tenor of critical inquiry and demanded the responsiveness of those in power.

Granted, students have not yet inquired into "the discourse of student need" (Horner 2015) as reform's warrant for neoliberal standardization. Still, we have good reason to seek out and anticipate resonances between student concerns and the claims of reform. Reform groups insist that standardization-for-competition will democratize access to opportunity, and we professionals insist that our expert judgment in context ensures the democratic representation of our diverse publics. But students, and particularly our most vulnerable students, rarely have the opportunity to challenge or authorize these claims. Inviting local inquiry into the teaching, learning, and assessment envisioned by professionals and reformers can restore student voice to a debate stalemated between appeals to markets and professionalism. Inviting and circulating local public inquiry may not safeguard us against deprofessionalization by reform, but what this proposal gives up in safety, I argue, it gains in participatory potential. By scaling down to local experience and scaling up to institutional, community, state, and national reform discussions, we might begin to draw on the participatory energy of public inquiry to support the professional goal of improving the discourse of reform.

This turn suggests a way to bring two of composition's central efforts into conversation with each other. That is, going public would draw on the resources of public engagement. Following Jeffrey Grabill's (2012) methodology of community research, we would attend to the ways student groups assemble publics through the creation of things (194) and the ways these assemblages invite or disinvite participation in public discussion (196). We would attend to these acts of public-making with the aim of helping students bring new publics into being (197). As institutional insiders, we would seek to help students work with existing discourses (199) that enable valuable kinds of activity (200) with specific materials

(201). In context, this would mean that we could guide students' inquiry into institutional reforms dealing with writing amid K–16 reform. But as non-students, we would also seek to understand how the stance and tenor of student engagement sponsors public discussion in ways that conventional professional rhetoric has not. This methodological stance describes the vision of this book: we can help our students sponsor public engagement around the question of publicness in teaching, learning, and assessing writing.

Put differently, we would become curators of public experience with literacy. The authorizing grounds for this role come from Linda Flower's (2008, 216–17) *Community Literacy*:

> the privileged become empowered to speak by becoming able to speak for the hidden agency of marginalized, silenced, or disempowered others . . . It is the caring, patiently precise, and writerly work of drawing out, documenting, and giving visibility and presence to the agency of someone else (in their own eyes and the eyes of others) when that person is presumed to lack such capacity, insight, or expertise. In this rhetoric of engagement, students and educators become rhetorical agents by seeing, supporting, and giving a public presence to the agency, capacity, ability, and insight of community partners. Such engagement takes different forms, from supporting to documenting to public fashioning.

In this light, our role would become helping our students create counterpublics around their literacy experiences. The shift here is that I am concerned with composition's professionalism amid reform; Flower is not. In recognizing the potential of an antiprofessional rhetoric of professionalism, however, I am *not* arguing that we abandon the professional publics we attend to by attempting to redirect reform or reassert professionalism. Rather, I am arguing that we expand our rhetoric of professionalism to engage the antiprofessional energy fostered by students' inquiry, circulation, and participation. With our appeals to professionalism frequently ignored by institution-, system-, and state-level administrators tasked with implementing K–16 reforms, we need an alternate basis for the authority of our judgment. One potential basis is the public participation of our students.

To develop this public rhetoric of professionalism, I recover the antiprofessional commitments of the pragmatic tradition that tend to be marginalized by efforts to reappropriate the rhetorics of reform or to reassert professional judgment. I then use these commitments as lenses through which to envision a participatory tactic of going public—a way of inviting critical public inquiry into the teaching, learning, and assessment envisioned by groups like Complete College America. Even if CCA ends up not being our primary concern in a few years, our challenges will be similar. We will still need to innovate on going public to counter our deprofessionalization by neoliberal reform.

THE EXIGENCIES OF GOING PUBLIC

The contemporary moment has a long history. Much scholarship explores how the rhetoric of reform tends to displace the professional judgment of literacy educators, as in the case of the Committee of Ten (Marshall 1995), "Johnny Can't Write" (Suhor 1994), *A Nation at Risk* (Varnum 1986), K–12 National Standards (Mayher 1990, 1999; Myers 1994), the Boyer Report (Marshall 2004), *No Child Left Behind* (Gallagher 2007), the Common Core (O'Neill et al. 2012), and the Collegiate Learning Assessment (Haswell 2012). I trace composition's current rhetorical exigency, however, to the 2009 emergence of the Common Core, which introduced not only an argument for K–12 standards and assessments but also a rhetorical style template for contemporary educational reform. This template was not new in 2009, but the Common Core refined reform's familiar appeals for the current moment. In this style, the world represents a warrant for reform, and in this world, the only viable policy choice is to standardize and centralize educational judgment: "today we live in a world without borders. To maintain America's competitive edge, we need all of our students to be well prepared and ready to compete with not only their American peers, but with students from around the world. These common standards will be a critical first step to bring about real and meaningful transformation of our education system to benefit all students" (Common Core State Standards 2008). Today, this style has been taken up by Complete College America and the Collegiate Learning Assessment. As these groups argue, global competition demands improved *college* readiness, completion, and outcomes for all students. To assess and improve performance across institutions and contexts, the goals and measures of literacy education must be common. Implied by this argument is a market model of public policy: since teachers and scholars refuse to standardize, policy development itself must become competitive. That way state leaders can invest in policy providers who best define what students need to succeed in the global marketplace. Such choice is not only economic: as the opening anecdote of this chapter demonstrates, reform frames market choice as the driver of *democratic* change. For students, parents, and state leaders, choosing among policy providers *is* public engagement, and this engagement is the driver of equity and justice.

As the 2016 CCCC theme attests, taking action in response to these appeals is composition's current public concern, but conceptualizing rhetorical innovation for public action has also been an ongoing disciplinary concern. In attempts to elaborate a standard of professional rhetorical judgment suited to the challenges of going public, composition scholars have appealed to pragmatism. Scholars have invoked this value to argue that defenses of our professional standing cannot simply decry reform amid the material, political, and rhetorical constraints surrounding professionalism. Over the last twenty years, most invocations of pragmatism have underwritten the argument that teachers and scholars can account for these constraints by working *from* the discourse of markets, whether at the institutional level or in the political sphere of education reform. For example, proponents of a bureaucratic or managerial pragmatism suggest that if institutional or political reforms value standardization, we can leverage this value to get better material support for students and instructors (R. Miller 1998a; R. Miller 1998b; White 2010; White 1991). Similarly, proponents of reframing argue that if reform demands students better

prepared for global competition, we can redirect this emphasis to build on our pluralistic judgment (Adler-Kassner 2008;
Adler-Kassner and Harrington 2010; Adler-Kassner and O'Neill
2010; Fleckenstein 2008). As I noted in the introduction, these
innovations invoke pragmatism not only to authorize their own
rhetorical judgment but also to discipline alternate judgments.
While these scholars recognize professional critiques of reform
as first steps toward going public, their conclusions are clear:
critique must give way to alternate strategies better suited to the
profound constraints of the contemporary context.

This is not to say that the rhetorical disciplining of bureaucracy or reframing has gone uncontested. As scholars of writing
program administration and assessment have argued, these innovations on going public tend toward their own consequences: a
pragmatism of reappropriation and redirection can limit composition to a "management theory of agency" (Bousquet 2003,
26) and subordinate our local practice to externally imposed
ends (Gallagher 2012, 45). This pragmatism can also direct
our attention away from alternate goals of going public, such
as building solidarity with our publics (Bousquet 2003, 27) and
remaking rather than redirecting the globally competitive scene
of reform (Gallagher 2011). But while these counterstatements
have driven dialectic in composition's disciplinary discussions,
they remain largely unoperationalized in our practices of going
public. That, I argue, is because these critical perspectives invite
us to explore our rhetoric of professionalism from an alternate
vantage point. Against the largely *politically* pragmatic innovations of bureaucracy and reframing, these critiques recall a central text in the *philosophically* pragmatic tradition, John Dewey's
(1927) *The Public and Its Problems*.[8] For Dewey, the task of professionals facing displacement by markets is not to reappropriate
the conventionalized appeals of bureaucracy and markets but to
refashion professional judgment as responsiveness to the diverse
contexts of public experience. He cautions that "rule by an economic class may be disguised from the masses; rule by experts
could not be covered up. It could be made to work only if the
intellectuals became the willing tools of big economic interests.

Otherwise they would have to ally themselves with the masses, and that implies, once more, a share in government by the latter" (205–6).

In a similar vein, Bousquet (2003) and Gallagher (2011) urge us to read our professional standing as contingent on its publicness, not its viability within a managerial or a competitive logic. From this perspective, a democratic defense of professionalism must be adequate to public participation and engagement. In this spirit, the innovations of bureaucracy, reframing, and public engagement seek to articulate a public rhetoric of professionalism for composition. But as I have argued here, these innovations tend both to advance and stymie Dewey's aims: we embrace *and* limit the vision of a participatory expertise. To attend more fully to his democratic aim for going public, I attempt to elaborate Dewey's vision with a rhetorical style for composition teachers and scholars responding to reform.

Such an effort at rhetorical innovation recognizes going public as a negotiation between two contending aims. While defending professional standing against bureaucratic standardization and marketization is our primary concern, another equally pressing challenge is facilitating public participation in professional responses to reform. Our conventional defense of professionalism, in which the diversity of the world requires expert judgment in context, attends to the first concern but tends to envision little role for our publics beyond assent to expertise. Following Dewey's vision of public-professional collaboration, I envision an alternate rhetoric of expertise that would invite public inquiry into what is erased by calls for reform: students' experiences with writing that unsettle the single scene of global competition. Moreover, this rhetorical style would invite our publics to re-assess our professional judgment as responsiveness to public experience. Such a rhetoric wagers that the diversity of contexts, purposes, and practices in our publics' experiences with literacy can support, rather than discount, our pluralistic professionalism.

This methodological hope resonates with calls in composition to attempt public engagement as a means of improving educational policies, K–16 (Gallagher 2005; Gallagher

2007; Gallagher 2010; Gallagher 2011; Goldblatt 2007; Parks and Goldblatt 2000; Rose 1995; Rose 2009; Rose 2010). Chris Gallagher's (2011) "Being There" offers the most recent call for this method of engagement: instead of claiming stakeholder status amid the neoliberal scene of assessment, Gallagher argues, we should seek to remake the scene to reflect our primary agency. We can assert that "being there matters," and we can form networks of like-minded groups and organizations to affirm our situated judgment in debate. Yet as I argue below, this rhetorical innovation also has its likely limits: amid the stalemates of reform debate, "being there" tends to collapse into the conventional assertion of professionalism that the diversity of contexts for teaching, learning, and assessment requires professional judgment in context. In other words, while "being there" reasserts the local against the global, the local still tends to stand in for, rather than invite, public participation.

My effort is to complement bureaucracy, reframing, and public engagement by contributing an alternate rhetorical method of inviting and circulating accounts of public inquiry. Along the lines Dewey articulates, I describe opportunities for composition teachers, scholars, and administrators not only to assert the epistemic advantage of locality but also to perform the professional inquiry that forms our expertise. I elaborate an alternate rhetorical style that forwards acts of teaching, learning, and assessment and invites local public inquiry into these acts as a means of disclosing perspectives discounted by reform. The aim of this rhetorical shift is to make the grounds of professional judgment available for public participation in reform. Rather than defending our professional standing as the means of democratic public representation, this alternate tactic would dramatize the grounds of our professional judgment for public assessment and authorization.

This approach to critique has a rhetorical aim that is, in Kenneth Burke's (1969a, 43) words, "neither a form of relativism nor a form of eclecticism." That is, my aims with this style are broader than disclosing a multiplicity of possible perspectives on an act of literacy teaching, learning, or assessment.

Rather, I am seeking to disclose these perspectives in order to highlight the realities omitted or marginalized by standardization-for-competition-for-democracy. An alternate style is a way of forwarding these realities to sponsor public recalcitrance (Burke 1984a, 47), a desire for reforms to develop terms adequate to reflect diverse experiences with the teaching, learning, and assessment of literacy. By inviting public participation and dissent, an alternate style attempts to shift the conventional relationship between composition's rhetorical means and its democratic ends of going public. Rather than asserting professionalism's conventional link between experts and expertise, an alternate style imagines public participation as composition's means of pursuing the democratic aim of pluralism.

THE RHETORICAL STYLES OF MARKETS, PROFESSIONALISM, AND DEMOCRACY

This proposal recognizes reform debate as a stalemate between two distinctive rhetorical styles. Reform enacts what rhetorical scholars of political economy call "realist style": proponents simultaneously invoke the competitive world as a warrant for one policy action while discounting alternate approaches as failing to grasp the world as it is (Asen 2009a, 14; Aune 2002, 42; Hariman 1995, 18; Hirschman 1970; Hirschman 1991). This style has clear political consequences in reform debate: it allows reformers to displace the professional standing of composition professionals who would otherwise claim privileged standing in the development of educational policy. But a realist style also has public consequences. By figuring public policy as mere accommodation to the world, and by defining that world as irreducibly competitive, realist style reduces the scope of public policy values to competition, efficiency, and instrumentality (Aune 2002, 36–37). Beyond the professional concerns of reform, then, market discourse is also a public concern because it "corrodes the persuasive norms that are the ground of republican culture" (Hariman 1995, 47) and undermines the democratic process of persuasion and deliberation (Aune 2002, 42).

In response to reform's realist style, we in composition tend to employ a contending style. We argue that the diversity of contexts for teaching and learning writing requires professional judgment in context. We forward professionalism as *the* means of democratically representing our diverse publics. This is our appeal, to be sure, but it is not unique; political theorists recognize this style as the quintessential rhetoric of professionalism. In Eliot Freidson's terms, we professionals conventionally assert that our "judgment resists standardization, commodification, or reduction to mechanical processes" (Freidson 2001, 17). What sets us apart from bureaucrats and market share-seekers is not just our expertise but our "devotion to a transcendent value which infuses [our] specialization with a larger and putatively higher goal which may reach beyond that of those [we] are supposed to serve" (122). When we defend our professional standing, then, we are concerned with asserting our "devotion to the use of disciplined knowledge and skill for the public good" (217), and to serve this good fully, we insist upon our independence. We claim a "duty to appraise what [we] do in light of that larger good, a duty which licenses [us] to be more than passive servants of the state, of capital, of the firm, of the client, or even of the immediate general public" (217).

In Burke's terms, this style's orientation is "idealist" (Burke 1969a, 128–31): while we may define the *scene* of teaching and learning as diverse and draw on the *agency* or means of research, we insist that the public good cannot be served without us, a designated class of *agents*. In reform debate, this dramatic resolution of terms plays a key role: as political theorist Magali Sarfatti Larson (1977) argues, this style allows professionals to figure their services as "inextricably bound to the person and personality of the producer," thus "constitut[ing] and control[ling] a market for their expertise" (xvi). If reform aims to improve teaching and learning, our rhetoric of professionalism insists that the goals and measures of literacy education cannot be defined by other agents such as testing corporations or political think tanks. Only *we* can make expert judgment on behalf of the public. Thus reform efforts seeking to improve teaching and learning must work through professionals with the understanding that our expert judgment is pluralistic and contextual and incompatible with the standardization of bureaucracy or the consumer choice of markets.

Like reformers' realist style, however, professionals' idealist style also has public consequences. When we go public, our stories resolve predictably: the scenes, agents, and purposes of literacy education *always* resolve to professional judgment in context. This appeal secures our professional standing but tends to offer our publics a narrow role in discussions of reform: assenting to our monopoly on expertise. As sociologist and political theorist Albert Dzur (2008) argues, professionals' style tends to elevate themselves to the status of "trustees" (45) who "work *for* the public but not *with* the public" (75). The problem with this rhetorical self-elevation is that it imagines little use for public participation in shaping and authorizing professional judgment.

In *The Public*, Dewey (1927) puts this critique more strongly: "no government by experts in which the masses do not have the chance to inform the experts as to their needs can be anything but an oligarchy managed in the interests of the few" (208). To create a collaborative model of expertise, Dewey argues, experts must do more than *assert* the publicness of their judgment. Instead, experts must improve "the methods and conditions of debate, discussion and persuasion." As Dewey imagines it, the role of experts shifts from making judgment on behalf of the public to sponsoring local public inquiry into shared issues and then circulating accounts of this inquiry beyond the original context (153). This circulation, in turn, can invite other publics to examine local concerns in light of ongoing inquiries elsewhere. By drawing on local knowledge and circulating accounts of it to inform broader conversations, Dewey argues, experts can develop collaborative relationships with their publics (205) and potentially earn trust in their judgment. Scaling down to local public experience through inquiry becomes a means of scaling up to the political economy of expertise.

These perspectives on reform's realist style and professionalism's idealist style highlight a similar tension: both rhetorics tend to minimize democratic public participation in the formation of policy. My concern in this book is with the ways that composition's central innovations on going public address the probable democratic consequences of these rhetorical styles. The innovations of bureaucracy and reframing, I argue, encourage us in composition to bracket rather than contend with the potential public consequences of realist style. While reappropriating and redirecting the bureaucratic and market discourses of reform can advance our professional judgment under constraint, these strategies also tend to entrench the real of realist style—the implacably competitive world as a warrant for foreclosing public participation in debate about educational reform. With this critique, however, I am *not* arguing that the innovations of bureaucracy and reframing lack concern for the democratic consequences of realist style. Instead, I am arguing that these innovations forward a standard of pragmatic judgment that encourages us in composition to define the scope of going public as achieving material and policy consequences (means) that can serve our democratic ends. The point of going public, in other words, becomes advancing professionalism so that professionals can advance democratic access. This orientation is the concern of Dewey and contemporary theorists of the political economy of professionalism. I draw out this concern in order to read bureaucracy and reframing adjacently—that is, with a critical eye toward their rhetorical style and its likely public consequences.

The innovation of public engagement, by contrast, attempts to enlarge the scope of going public by reversing the prevailing means-ends judgment. Rather than defending professionalism to improve democracy, a strategy of public engagement seeks to improve democracy to defend professionalism: proponents invite participation in the hope that a greater public role will unsettle reform's appeal of standardization for competition and improve public discourse about writing. In this sense, the innovation of public engagement aligns with my argument in this book. Yet my positioning alongside public engagement still seeks opportunities to extend its potential. I have argued that the appeal of "being there," despite its emphasis on the locality of experience and contingent judgment, still tends, amid the stalemates of reform debate, to collapse into the conventional appeal of professionalism: the contingency of the world requires expert judgment in context. While this rhetoric of public engagement critically conceptualizes the publics formed by realist style, I argue, it only partly addresses the publics formed by idealist style.

As pragmatic innovations on going public, both the reappropriation and redirection of reform and the reassertion of professionalism advance composition's efforts to contend with Dewey's goad toward public professionalism. And yet these innovations also tend to close down the avenues that Dewey seeks to open. My emphasis here is on *tending*: these critiques are not certainties by any means, but they are attempts to envision the probable consequences of our rhetorical judgment. To account more fully for Dewey's vision, I argue, is to expand on the redirection of reform's realist style and the reassertion of professionalism's idealist style. In this book, I seek to complement these strategies by envisioning a potentially public rhetoric of professionalism, one that features multiple grounds of educational judgment—in the terms of Burke's (1969a) pentad, the acts, the scenes, the agencies, the purposes, and the agents of teaching and learning. With this broader set of appeals, I aim to create alternate opportunities for our publics to affirm the publicness of professional judgment.

PRAGMATIC RHETORICAL INNOVATION

As the current reform arguments suggest, however, public debates are deeply stalemated over definitions of the scene, agency, purpose, and agent of education. The 2009 exchange between the Common Core and the National Council of Teachers of English (NCTE) (Bomer et al. 2009) dramatizes these standoffs. Should the *scene* of literacy education be understood as global and single, as reformers insist, or diverse and local, as we argue? Should the *agency* or means of education be standardized or pluralistic?

Should the policy *agent* be any service provider, or must the agent be a designated professional? And, should the *purpose* be competitiveness or democratic preparation? Amid these calcified struggles over policy meaning, composition teachers, scholars, and administrators would appear to have little room for invention. Hence the appeal of bureaucratic innovation: if the only viable agency or policy in the contemporary scene is standardization, at least it can be standardization that reflects our participation. And, hence the innovation of reframing: if the only viable scene is the globally competitive, at least this can be a diverse world that requires our pluralistic judgment. Public engagement attempts a different kind of innovation, one that seeks to shift the scene: if reform's scene is global, then the scene of professionalism must be contextual and feature agents making judgment in context. Thus "being there matters" for teaching, assessment, and learning; thus local judgment in context must be preserved to serve the public good. In this light, the only agent who can enact this local judgment is the professional.

While these innovations focused on scene and agency make productive use of the available means in debate, they tend to marginalize an avenue for rhetorical invention. A term rarely featured in realist or idealist style is *act.* That is, in efforts to make arguments at the policy level, reformers and professionals tend to avoid emphasizing specific acts of teaching and learning. For reformers, the competitive global scene encompasses all factors and determines policy; for us in composition, expert agents reflect all factors and determine policy. In this standoff, acts of teaching and learning are subsumed within the emphases on scene or agent. To emphasize acts in going public, then, is to depart from the conventions of reform debate.[9] But Burke's alternate realist perspective suggests that performing our inquiry into acts can serve an important role in going public by disclosing a range of factors often cropped out of reform debate: the scenes in which an act takes place, the agents who act, these agents' purposes, and the means with which these agents act. This disclosing function describes the dynamic of conversations

Maja Wilson and I had with parents: public inquiry into acts of writing restored pluralism to discussions otherwise narrowed by reform's neoliberalism or professionalism's preservation of expertise. This inquiry also lent us grounds for breaking, if only momentarily, from composition professionals' rhetorical habit of calcifying the existing stalemates of reform debate.

Like the realist style of reform and the idealist style of professionalism, an alternate realist style also has its likely consequences. It attempts to fashion professionalism less as a monopoly on expertise and more as an effort to facilitate public engagement that may affirm, correct, or qualify expert perspectives. Monopoly is a fighting word, to be sure, but it reflects what political theorists consider *the* basis of professionalism. As Freidson (2001) argues, "those specializations which embody values held by the public at large, the state, or some powerful elite are given the privileged status of monopoly, or control over their own work. *This monopolistic control is the essential characteristic of . . . professionalism from which all else flows*" (32; emphasis in original). While I recognize that composition teachers, scholars, and administrators have a tenuous relationship with professionalism (Horner 2000), and that faculty are increasingly "managed professionals" in the contemporary university (Rhoades 1998; Rhoades 2007), our efforts at going public continue to appeal to what Freidson calls "the essential characteristic" of professionalism: the public good of maintaining the exclusivity of our expertise.[10]

A participatory vision of professionalism, however, would shift the practice of going public closer to an antiprofessional mode of public engagement, Burke's (1984a) comic critique. Rather than envisioning themselves outside the dialectic of perspectives, Burke argues, comic critics recognize themselves as participants in a larger drama: "when you add that people are necessarily mistaken, that all people are exposed to situations in which they must act as fools, that every insight contains its own special kind of blindness, you complete the comic circle, returning again to the lesson of humility that underlies great tragedy" (41). In this drama, Burke argues, "debunking" contending perspectives may be useful for "polemical and disintegrative purposes" (93) but it is not helpful for "transcendence upward," or for envisioning more encompassing terms and perspectives adequate to reflecting the experiences of a greater range of participants in debate.

To pursue this goal of enlarging the discourse of debate, Burke argues, critics need not only share the "bureaucratization" (246) of their perspectives—their favored terms for their values—but also foster the *experiences* of inquiry and critique that can dramatize the grounds for these values. This broader aim lends discussion and debate a sense of "wholeness." When a critique is too "efficient," meaning that it seeks the establishment of a certain set of terms *more* than a fulsome dialectic among perspectives, it endangers the sense of comic fallibility that can unite proponents of clashing views (248–50). From this perspective, an enlarging criticism is one that does not resolve too quickly or reliably to a favored vocabulary. This delayed resolution to calcified terms is the aim of an alternate realist style. Rather than immediately resolving policy questions to the professional agent, the aim of this style is to foreground the factors—the scenes, agents, agencies, and purposes encompassed by an act—cropped out of reform. Rather than asserting professionalism as the democratic representation of our diverse publics, an alternate realist style attempts to foster public participation as a means of constructing a more democratically adequate set of terms for literacy education.

This approach suggests a rhetoric and sociology of professionalism that departs from the conventional in composition. As Giles Gunn (1988) notes, a comic critique seeks not to reclose debate around a favored set of terms but to restore to a conversation the elements excluded (72). This comic aim does not allow us to escape from the imperative to defend professionalism but rather helps us find "transcendence" (79) within that imperative. That transcendence, Gunn argues, is remaining "supple and quixotic enough to resist the seductions even of [our] own performance." In other words, "to be fully effective in resisting the pull of its own pieties, our criticism must reflect what Burke calls 'our fundamental kinship with the enemy'" (82). In rhetorical terms, this means we in composition would recognize our reliance as professionals on idealist style as parallel to reformers' reliance on realist style. These vocabularies make up the available means for professionals and reformers to advance competing social logics amid the political economy of reform. At the same time, both rhetorics represent what Burke (1984b) calls "trained incapacities" for public engagement. Realist and idealist style tend to work against the public participation both Burke and Dewey envision as central to democratic professionalism. In a comic mode, going public would seek to foreground the failures of conventional rhetorics of expertise to represent public experience and point toward an alternate, more adequate rhetoric—one that, of course, we *hope* will feature the contributions of professionals. But the difference between a comic critique and a conventional rhetoric of professionalism is the role of public participation. In Burke's antiprofessional vision, professional judgment is authorized through public participation and dissent.

This openness to public inquiry and participation may seem implausible for composition professionals amid the present scene of reform. While many of us acknowledge that our professional perspectives are selective and limited, few of us acknowledge in reform debate that our judgment is "necessarily mistaken"; fewer still emphasize our "fundamental kinship" with reformers. Even scholars advocating public engagement rarely frame going public as *our* opportunity to revise perspectives. But Burke's comic stance poses a trenchant challenge regarding our purpose in professional critiques of reform: is it to move the dialectic upward, discovering more encompassing terms that can enable broader participation? Or is the purpose to move the dialectic downward toward narrower terms that allow for professional power through control?

Burke's perspective goads us toward the former and against the latter. As David Blakesley (1999) reads Burke, the task of "resourceful critics and artists" facing stalemated debates becomes "cultivat[ing] alternative perspectives by shifting the 'vocabulary of approach'" (71). But Burkean dialectic does more than disrupt—it also offers a resource for our rhetorical innovation on idealist style. This rhetorical judgment and action recognizes that a comic stance has the potential to move the dialectic upward. It attempts to restore what Burke (1969b) calls a "babel of voices" to discussions narrowed by dominant perspectives. Such rhetorical disruption may sound promising at a time when reform's appeals to standardization-for-competition-for-democracy appear to be displacing our professional claims to expertise. Yet the specific stance of criticism Burke seeks is not all outwardly aimed; on the contrary, M. Elizabeth Weiser (2008) argues, the comic frame places the critic—and especially the *professional* critic—among the world of necessarily mistaken perspectives. By seeking to recreate a new babel, Burke suggests that critics can forge a new unity, a more encompassing or transcendent one that can reflect merger and division (127). This unity is ironic, Weiser admits, but the experience of forging a cooperative vision is the "transcendence of the conversation," the opportunity to "[find] the level at which perspectives seemingly in opposition can be merged to determine the best aspects of each and the manner in which each is 'pervaded by the spirit' of the other" (131). The payoff of a comic critique is the potential for a fuller dialectic among participants in debate rather than the establishment of professional authority.

For composition's efforts at going public, a comic critique charts a departure from the judgment informing the rhetorical innovations of bureaucracy and reframing. Rather than separating composition's rhetorical means and democratic ends, a comic critique seeks to rejoin these means and ends. Like the innovation of public engagement, a comic critique seeks to form publics based on local inquiry, but a comic critique also extends the aims of public engagement beyond the defense of professionalism. For Burke, the purpose of professional critique is to facilitate the maturation of perspectives so that they can encompass the broadest and fullest participation of all involved. This is the democratic challenge that Burke's and Dewey's pragmatic inquiries pose to the practice of going public. How can we in composition foster the kind of democratic dialectic that we value in public spheres while also contending with the threat of our own professional displacement amid neoliberal reform? In the next chapters, I explore how our existing innovations on going public have taken up this challenge.

CHAPTER SUMMARIES

The historical arc of this book begins in the late 1990s and early 2000s when a set of scholars began to question the capacity of professionals' critiques to account for the material constraints of institutional life (R. Miller 1998a; R. Miller 1998b; Porter et al. 2000; J. Harris 1997). In the place of critique, these scholars advocated a qualified embrace of the prevailing rhetoric of institutional power, standardization, an embrace that has since been termed bureaucracy or managerialism (Bousquet 2003; Strickland 2011). While these scholars focus on institutional and administrative contexts, I explore their arguments because their conceptions of pragmatic rhetorical innovation inform present efforts to address the constraints of national reform.

In chapter 2, I analyze arguments for a bureaucratic pragmatism of going public. This pragmatism questions two rhetorical conventions among composition professionals: critiquing the democratic limits of standardizing institutional and political reforms, and invoking the transcendent democratic good of professionals' pluralistic judgment. Instead of following these conventions, proponents of a bureaucratic pragmatism encourage composition teachers, scholars, and administrators to reassess the potential use of the discourses of their contexts for democratic ends. Here bureaucracy engages with a key concern in the philosophically pragmatic tradition, the fashioning of rhetorical ends-in-view (Dewey 1935) as strategies to address specific consequences (James 1907). But I argue that the rhetorical innovation of bureaucracy tends to emphasize one form of consequences— the material benefits we can gain from appropriating the dominant discourses in our institutional and political contexts. While this emphasis on the material is framed as necessary to deliver democratic goods, I explore how the rhetorical discipline associated with material consequences tends to limit our pursuit of an equally central consequence in the philosophically pragmatic tradition—namely, inviting public participation in authorizing professional judgment. Based on this critique, I reconsider the institutional and professional concerns of a bureaucratic rhetoric within the broader public context of contemporary reform. With standardization now serving as a means for marketization in contemporary reform, I argue that composition's rhetoric of professionalism needs to address not only bureaucratic concerns but also those of public engagement.

In chapter 3, I explore the recent period of 2008–12 when a set of scholars began to take up themes central to the earlier discussion of bureaucracy: the seeming futility of professional critiques to effect policy change and the necessity of tactical rhetorical action to redirect reforms framed by market discourse (Adler-Kassner 2008; Adler-Kassner and Harrington 2010; Adler-Kassner and O'Neill 2010; Fleckenstein 2008). Unlike scholars advocating a rhetoric of bureaucracy, scholars forwarding reframing identify themselves not with managerialism but with democratic activism. As I argue in this chapter, however, the innovation of reframing urges a similar rhetorical discipline for professionals going public: teachers', scholars', and administrators' task is to reappropriate and redirect the dominant discourse of reform, but in the national sphere rather than in the institutional setting. To guide this rhetorical judgment, proponents of reframing invoke two key pragmatic aims: melioration, or the improvement of public discourse, and Cornel West's (1989) "prophetic pragmatism," a "form of cultural criticism that attempts to transform linguistic, social, cultural, and political traditions for the purposes of increasing the scope of individual development and democratic operations" (230). Yet I argue that the practice of reframing is likely both to advance and foreshorten these aims. By envisioning pragmatic melioration as the redirection of existing policy arguments, reframing discourages composition's attention to the antidemocratic consequences of reform's realist style. And in its effort to manage professionals' public critiques of reform, reframing minimizes opportunities for our non-expert publics to inquire into and respond critically to reform. To expand reframing's pragmatism for going public, I reconsider the potential of professional critique to be "artful"—that is, to account for local public experiences with reform. I take the possibility of an artful critique as a reminder that going public can not only defend professionalism but also foster forms of public participation that can authorize professional judgment as publicly representative. To illustrate such critical participation, I describe current opportunities for going public on the issue of machine scoring.

In chapter 4, I examine a set of arguments that began developing in the 1990s but have taken on a new urgency in the contemporary era of reform (Gallagher 2005; Gallagher 2007; Gallagher 2010; Gallagher 2011; Goldblatt 2007; Parks and Goldblatt 2000; Rose 1995; Rose 2009; Rose 2010). These perspectives, which I term public engagement, attempt a rhetorical departure from the pragmatism of reframing and bureaucracy. Rather than disciplining critique or advocating the redirection of institutional and political commonplaces, public engagement envisions an alternate rhetoric of professionalism. This rhetoric is aimed at unsettling the decline narratives of education reform. This aim—what Dewey (1927, 168) terms breaking up "conventionalized consciousness"—calls on composition teachers, scholars, and administrators to sponsor public inquiry into teaching and learning *and* to circulate accounts of this inquiry as a means of improving public discourse and potentially building public trust in professional judgment. Where public engagement can be extended, I argue, is in its elaboration of professionals' rhetorical practice. While scholars seek to represent public perspectives on literacy education, the favored rhetorical style of going public tends to remain "idealist": that is, to represent the diversity of public experiences with literacy, we should preserve professional standing to define the goals and measures of public education. Rhetorically, this style risks reducing public participation to the act of assenting to expertise. To engage more fully with the antiprofessional energy of pragmatic inquiry, I recognize public engagement as a search for an alternate style—a rhetorical means of returning reform debate to local, experiential contexts and facilitating public participation in reform. I conclude by envisioning such a response to college outcomes assessments like the Collegiate Learning Assessment. In chapter 5, I explore the consequences of adopting an alternate style for going public. I argue that such a rhetoric of professionalism helps us pursue the pragmatic aims highlighted in this book: attending to consequences, improving public discourse, and facilitating public participation. In that sense, an alternate realist style offers us a resource for composition's rhetorical innovation amid reform. Yet an alternate realist style also presents a goad: it invites us into dissenting modes of going public, it commits us to rhetorical circulation outside our professional spheres, and it opens up our own professionalism to critical inquiry. These likely consequences remind us that teachers, scholars, and administrators seeking to foster public participation in reform are not only engaging in rhetorical but also sociological innovation. And with this innovation comes an ethical question about professionals' roles in circulating public experiences of inquiry. Whose interests are we serving? While the circulation of public inquiry unsettles our role as curators of publics experience with literacy, I defend an alternate realist style as a means of expanding, rather than closing down, public participation in reform debate. An alternate realist style begins to reconcile the defense of professionalism with the sponsoring of public participation against the tide of contemporary reform.

NOTES

1. These arguments dramatize the tension between what economist Albert Hirschman (1970) calls voice and choice as models of public education reform. Corporate-political reforms emphasize consumer choice (and market competition) as a mechanism for improving teaching and learning while professional models praise public voice and participation as the primary means of improvement. Like Hirschman, I embrace voice as a democratic principle but also recognize the role of rhetorical critics in "bringing out the hidden potential of whatever . . . is currently neglected" (126) in debate. Given the dominant role of choice in con-

temporary reform, I make the case for professionalism as a mechanism for voice. However, I argue that the first step in making professionalism a mechanism for public voice is to develop an alternate rhetoric of professionalism, one suited to inviting public engagement.

2. I explore bureaucracy, markets, and professionalism as rhetorics for social logics. A bureaucratic social logic defines consistency and efficiency as the public goods that can be delivered by public policy. Accordingly, a rhetoric of bureaucracy appeals to these goods against the goods of consumer choice forwarded by proponents of markets and contextualism forwarded by proponents of professionalism. The clash among these appeals is stalemated because—as political theorist Eliot Freidson (2001) argues—public faith in the image of each of these logics drives policy choices as much as or more than the content of policy itself (3). To go public in composition, then, is to envision a *public* rhetoric of professionalism, a way of defending professionalism as a public good. To go public is to intervene in the rhetoric of political economy.

3. The American Association of Colleges and Universities' VALUE rubrics claim to offer "Valid Assessment of Learning in Undergraduate Education" (Association of American Colleges and Universities 2014). AAC&U is careful to emphasize the centrality of faculty in rubric development and the need to translate its rubrics into "the language of individual campuses, disciplines, and even courses."

4. The American Diploma Project (ADP) foresaw how the National Governors Association could channel the corporate-political platforms of groups like Achieve, Inc. to state leaders, who would adopt this platform as public policy, thus bypassing legislative and public review. Compare, for example, Achieve's 2004 *Ready or Not* (Achieve, Inc. 2004) to the NGA's 2005 *Action Agenda* (Achieve, Inc., and National Governors Association 2005): like the American Legislative Exchange Council (ALEC), the NGA publicizes corporate-political platforms.

5. Students at Northwestern University sparked national discussion of the "amateur" status of athletes. University of Missouri students thrust into the national spotlight the question of institutions' role in achieving racial justice. And students at Columbia University (and elsewhere) dramatized the need for public discussion of sexual violence.

6. The *Columbia Tribune* has published the October 2015 demands of Concerned Student 1950 (Concerned Student 1950 2015).

7. Counterpublic resistance is mostly commonly understood as the practice of subaltern groups petitioning the state for rights. But as Robert Asen (2009b) points out, members of the conservative intelligentsia embraced a counterpublic strategy in the 1970s to consolidate power against a perceived liberal hegemony. Following Asen, I understand counterpublic resistance as a group's performance of marginality and exclusion that aims to construct an ethos of gaining access to public debate. This performance is Concerned Student 1950's central rhetorical resource: performances of exclusion drive local action, motivate the digital and rhetorical circulation of these local actions, and sponsor parallel efforts

elsewhere. This cycle of action resembles what Asen and Brouwer (2001) call a "public modality," a productive practice through which counterpublic groups engage each other and institutions in a process of change.

8. As I discuss in chapters 2 and 3, proponents of bureaucracy and reframing invoke the philosophically pragmatic aims of attending to consequences and prophetic melioration. These proponents enact these aims rhetorically by reappropriating standardization and redirecting competition. But these rhetorical enactments also limit these pragmatic aims. That is why I read bureaucracy and reframing as "largely politically pragmatic" innovations. Their rhetorical performances attend to the concerns of the consequences foregrounded in the politically pragmatic tradition (policy and the material) while also marginalizing those emphasized in the philosophically pragmatic tradition—the public-forming functions of rhetoric, the role of critical public participation in democracy (Festenstein 1997). Despite this reading, my analysis does not aim to discount bureaucracy's and reframing's contributions to going public so much as anticipate the consequences of their rhetorical choices. Based on my attention to these consequences, I have made a contestable judgment—that the rhetorical performances of bureaucracy and reframing both enable and undermine composition's capacity for public professionalism.

9. Burke (1969a, 128–31) terms an emphasis on act a realist perspective, but this perspective is not the same as reform's "realist style." Reformers invoke the globally competitive scene as a warrant for action and as a means of denying the need for alternate perspectives. Thus reform's realist style would more accurately be termed a "materialist" style since its drama invokes the world in order to *close* critical inquiry into the relationship between the world invoked and the policies proposed. Burke's realist perspective, by contrast, seeks to *reopen* critical inquiry into the relationship between the world invoked and policies proposed.

10. As sociologist Gary Rhoades (2007) argues, "professors have historically been conceptualized as professionals independent of the state" (120), yet "such a perspective overlooks the realities of the workplace and ignores another vantage point for considering the professions . . . all professors work in large organizations, where the scope of their autonomy is delimited by various sorts of managers" (121). In large organizations like the university, "more than one professional group operates" (127), which is to say that there are managerial professions. These managerial professionals are the fastest growing category of professional employment in higher education (128). "Simply put, though they may neither realize nor acknowledge it, professors are not the only professionals on campus" (129). Because the managerial professionals have neither academic freedom nor intellectual property rights, they are much more "closely connected to management" (130).

Chapter 2

BUREAUCRACY, "LIGHTNESS," AND DISCONTENT

The blanket rejection of educational standardization is undemocratic. To say that educational competence can't be judged by any standardized measure mystifies such competence by turning it into a matter of taste or whim—an ineffable je ne sais quoi *mysteriously possessed by a minority of superior talents—rather than a set of practices that can be identified, modeled, and made generally accessible. It's a short step from telling the Spellings Commission, "Sorry, but we colleges are just too diverse to be measured by any common standard," to telling* students, *"Sorry, but the basic skills that you need to succeed in college are just too complex and heterogeneous to be explained to you clearly."*

—Gerald Graff and Cathy Birkenstein,
"A Progressive Case for Academic
Standardization: How Not to Respond
to Calls for Common Standards" (2008, 219)

In "A Progressive Case," Graff and Birkenstein do not address composition teachers, scholars, and administrators directly. Rather, the authors call out college presidents and the American Association of Colleges and Universities for their "blanket rejection" (219) of standardization. But Graff and Birkenstein nevertheless engage composition's concerns when they invoke our central objection to standardized college outcomes assessments—that such measures don't reflect the diversity of contexts in which students write. Pointing to their *They Say, I Say* books, Graff and Birkenstein insist that our objection is mistaken. Common writing outcomes constitute "good standardization" (17) because they can increase democratic access to

DOI: 10.7330/9781607326540.c002

opportunity. By extension, we should not valorize professional rejections of standardization as productive engagements with reform; rather, we should recognize these rejections for what they are—"undemocratic" (219) refusals to serve our publics. With this admonition, Graff and Birkenstein urge writing professionals to adopt an alternate response to reform. From this moment forward, the authors suggest, *you* must speak for standardization as a means of democratization. This is an outsider exhortation, but its appeal is familiar within composition. As in our disciplinary debate over bureaucracy/ management, there is a split between competing standards of rhetorical judgment. Our conventional professional appeal to pluralism is well-established. Such pluralism, we argue, not only reflects our expert attention to context but also ensures the democratic representation of our diverse publics. Therefore, standardizing professional judgment imperils democracy. But unsettling this conventionality is a call for rhetorical innovation. This call, summarized in chapter 1 as a bureaucratic rhetoric of professionalism, proceeds from questions of definition to questions of value. The work of professionals is to uphold standards of good judgment, but because we hesitate to frame our expertise in standardizing terms, we suffer unfavorable consequences. We fail to steer emerging institutional and political reforms, and once these reforms have been implemented, we struggle to secure the material conditions that would ensure student access to opportunity. To serve our democratic aims, then, we need to innovate rhetorically, and that innovation means suspending our conventional appeal to the transcendent valence of pluralism and reclaiming the dominant language of institutional and political reform standardization.

Even though Graff and Birkenstein do not cite this debate, they echo the appeals of bureaucracy's proponents. To be clear, I am drawing no direct lineage from our scholarly conversation to Graff and Birkenstein's argument. The latter authors' standing is premised largely on their *non-belonging* to composition, a positioning which authorizes them to dismiss our central arguments without the burden of engaging us inside the profession.

But an outsideness to professionalism, and particularly an outsideness to our conventional rhetoric of professionalism, is what connects Graff and Birkenstein to calls for a rhetoric of bureaucracy originating from within the profession. Both claim a wisdom achievable only from outside the conventionality of our field. And based on this wisdom, both our disciplinary and our extra-disciplinary voices invite us in composition to attempt a similar form of innovation: adopting an alternate rhetoric suited to the contemporary context, be it institutional or national in scope.

This chapter explores how insiders might productively contend with this outsider innovation as we take up the theoretical and practical work of going public. I emphasize contending because Graff and Birkenstein's means-ends pragmatism is easy to dismiss within composition. Hope for "intelligent standardization" appears quixotic in 2016 when states' participation in K–16 articulation reforms has been politically secured above the level of our institutions and professions. Likewise, claiming managerial standing seems futile when the contemporary marketplace of policy expertise does not invite the contributions of writing teachers, scholars, and administrators.[1] With no apparent role for us to standardize in contemporary reform, we might see no reason to reconsider our appeals to pluralism. But even if this assessment is correct, it only partly engages the case for bureaucracy. Indeed, if their presentation at the 2016 CCCC is any indication, Graff and Birkenstein no longer argue that their pragmatism may enable us to reappropriate emerging reforms. Rather, Graff and Birkenstein insist that their innovation gets at something bigger: it recasts the relationship of professionalism to democracy. In their view, refashioning ourselves as service providers of standardization-for-democracy is the *best* we can do as professionals. When we innovate pragmatically, then, we are not simply getting by but actually doing *better* than those who insist on the conventional appeals of professionalism. We are bringing wisdom from the outside to the inside *for the public good.*

This, I believe, is the claim we should assess: how does a rhetoric of bureaucracy square its appeals to standardization with our ethical imperative to uphold democratic public representation (Mortensen 1998)? And to what extent does bureaucracy satisfy composition's ongoing search for a public rhetoric of professionalism? Graff and Birkenstein, like the other scholars discussed in this chapter, answer these questions by appealing to the pragmatism of their judgment. Such pragmatism attempts what philosopher Colin Koopman (2009, 197) calls the "melioration of problematic situations . . . fashioned on the basis of resources already furnished in that situation." Working from this orientation, Graff and Birkenstein call for writing professionals to set aside objections to the discourse of standardization in an attempt to reappropriate emerging reforms. At least then, they argue, we can achieve "intelligent standardization," and our efforts at going public can serve the democratic aims we invoke. If we suspend our professional appeals to pluralism, then, we can actually *better* serve the transcendent aim of this pluralism—the democratic representation of our diverse publics.

Read as pragmatic inquiry, Graff and Birkenstein's critique recognizes the limits of our conventional rhetoric of professionalism, which tends to reify rather than reopen the stalemates of reform debate. Moreover, Graff and Birkenstein point out how professionals' invocations of transcendent democratic possibilities tend to reduce public participation to one gesture—that of assent to our exclusive expertise. But while proponents of a bureaucratic pragmatism recognize the limits of composition's conventional appeals to pluralism, they say less about the democratic limits of their preferred discourse. In this chapter, I elaborate these limits, exploring how bureaucratic appeals can collapse into what Marc Bousquet (2003) calls "the rhetoric of an exclusive purchase on reality" (25). That is, the case for intelligent standardization assures writing professionals that the world demands management, and the best we can do is to work within managerial terms *if* we want to serve democratic access for our students. When addressed to our publics and particularly our students, a rhetoric of standardization limits conversation in similar ways: if you want democratic access to opportunity, you must accept standardization and set aside your concerns about diversity, contexts, and difference. Cropped out of this rhetorical and political vision, however, is the possibility that professional appeals to pluralism can sponsor critical public participation in reform debate.

As a potentially public rhetoric, then, bureaucracy narrows the grounds of our professionalism. Still, by challenging us to reconsider our rhetoric of professionalism, proponents of bureaucracy usefully undertake what Robert Hariman (1989) calls the rhetoric of inquiry: they open our professional rhetorical practice to critical examination and perform an alternate rhetoric in the hope of securing different consequences in the world. My aim is to highlight the contributions of this inquiry and critique, even if my larger conclusion is to temper its innovations. My approach is to consider the hoped-for consequences of going bureaucratic alongside other potential consequences of reappropriating appeals to standardization. Based on this inquiry, I reassess bureaucratic innovation in light of its larger aim. I argue that bureaucracy's innovation assumes that our publics seek our management. But if our publics are seeking other relationships to writing professionals, and I believe they are, we will need to attempt other innovations on going public.

BUREAUCRACY AS AN INNOVATION ON
THE DEFENSE OF PROFESSIONALISM

Conventionally, bureaucratic or managerial reforms forward governmental mechanisms for standardizing teaching, learning, and assessment. As political theorist Eliot Freidson (2001) argues, managerial control seeks out not specialized professionals but generalists who can apply best practices consistently across contexts (116). In contemporary K–16 reform, however, testing corporations and political think thanks have superseded governmental organizations as the agents who define the goals and measures of public education in literacy. These non-governmental groups' common standards and assessments allow for comparisons of test scores across states and contexts, and these comparisons enable service providers to compete for roles usually protected by conventional professional standing. In political-economic terms, the conventional three-way struggle among the social logics of professionalism, bureaucracy, and markets has collapsed into a two-way contest. Bureaucratic standardization now enables marketization, and marketization represents the primary alternative to professionalism as a means of democratizing access to educational opportunity. Although Freidson does not refer to the contemporary education reform scene, his observation applies: "the ideological assertion of economism . . . should be viewed as a frontal assault on professionalism" (218). In other words, when the value of public policy such as education is reduced to economic considerations, the professional pursuit of democratic aims is the first to be dismissed as cost-ineffective. In the present context, then, a call within composition to embrace a bureaucratic rhetoric may seem less like an innovation than a simple accommodation of the momentum toward markets.

That is not the view of the scholars surveyed in this chapter, however; they insist that a bureaucratic appeal can reflect composition's publics, the rhetorics suited to these publics, and the possibilities of our public rhetorical action. To be sure, these scholars focus on institutional contexts and do not engage the current moment of reform. But in their arguments, these scholars envision themselves accounting for and even thriving within the material, political, and rhetorical limitations of context. Where our denunciations of corporate values or appeals to democratic purpose have not been successful, a rhetoric of bureaucracy is imagined as a way of advancing our goals. In Kenneth Burke's pentadic terms, bureaucratic rhetorical judgment recognizes the limits of idealist style as a response to realist style. Rather than emphasize the conventional terms of professionalism, bureaucratic innovation enacts what Burke (1969a) calls a "pragmatic" orientation, locating expertise in the agency or means of public action, de-emphasizing the contextual judgment of professionals and calling attention to the consistency, efficiency, and reliability of professional knowledge. By going bureaucratic, this argument suggests, we may sacrifice some of the nuance afforded by contextual judgment *but at least we'd be the ones doing it.*

It is hard to imagine a composition teacher, scholar, or administrator who has articulated this rationale more memorably than Ed White. For White (1991), the embrace of bureaucracy is part of a broader rhetorical imperative. The social responsibility of WPAs, he argues, is to defend professional judgment using the means appropriate to the context (White 2010, 185). When addressing our public audiences, White suggests, there is no disinterested position from which we can defend ourselves, so we must learn to identify and exploit the available means of each context (188). This means, at times, simplifying our arguments despite the complexity of the issue (192). When working as administrators, we must be prepared to tailor our arguments to the specific institutional setting (White 1991, 6) and recognize that some—administrators, fellow faculty—won't respond to anything else but bureaucratic maneuvering (7–8). To deny this reality, White argues, would be to ignore the basic realities of institutional life. That is because the position of WPA "is one more or less under siege, and we had better take stock of the power arrayed against us, the power we have to fight for our programs, or we will not be doing our jobs. If we really don't want to deal in power, we had better step aside, or we will be doing more harm than good . . . If these metaphors sound overly military and Machiavellian, you are either new to administration, or you act instinctively in ways that you prefer not to recognize (6). White's imperative to use the language and structures of the institution have been termed as "White's Second Law of Assessodynamics" (Gallagher 2012, 57; Goldblatt 2007, 111–12), or "assess thyself or have assessment done unto you."

White is not addressing the current moment of reform debate, but he is making an argument about composition's rhetoric of professionalism. For White, a rhetoric of professionalism must be contextual. If our audiences want simple answers, we must be prepared to offer such answers; if our audiences want more nuanced perspectives, we should offer those as well. Broadly speaking, White suggests that we must suppress our conventional rhetoric of professionalism in favor of a more contextual one. White calls on us to set aside our conventional idealist style and adopt the discourse that is favored in the situation, most likely one emphasizing agency or policy. As a style, White's argument can be considered a form of realist-pragmatic appeal: the world is threatening and requires responses we are not conventionally prepared to give, but in the end, the world must dictate how we respond to reform. Therefore, we must learn to respond using the means appropriate to the situation. A pragmatic professionalism means subordinating one rhetoric of contextual judgment (idealist style) to another (the pragmatist accommodation to dominant discourse).

This is the argument of Richard Miller (1998a), except that Miller adds an additional critique. Not only is composition's rhetoric of professionalism properly centered on the "microbureaucratic" level of institutional practices (3), but we also need to stop responding to reforms in the terms we favor. We should stop talking about education as "emancipation" because such talk perpetuates the belief that the practice of teaching and learning is freedom from constraints (5). Critique, which Miller identifies as our favored response to reform, is dismissed as ineffective in securing real material benefits for teachers, administrators, and students. Rather than decry reforms or the constraints of institutionalized education, Miller suggests, we need to recognize an opportunity to use bureaucratic means to pursue democratic and equality-driven goals (40). Thus, Miller urges us to "go small" with goals (46), focusing on local and institutional publics (204) and working from composition's marginalized position (208) to deliver public goods.

Miller's argument is both do- and do-not: on the one hand, we need to learn to make the case that our judgment represents practical, bureaucratic management (even as it may pursue radical aims). At the same time, we need to stop critiquing reform on the basis of radical democratic values or liberatory themes. It is time, Miller argues, to "leave off critiquing the academy for having failed to make good on its promise to deliver a meaningful, morally sacrosanct life and to begin, instead, to work within the fiscal and bureaucratic constraints that both enable the academic enterprise and limit its scope" (210). For Miller, a realistic "politics of impurity" (9) would be based less on the radical critic/public intellectual than on the hybrid identity of the intellectual-bureaucrat (216; see also Miller 1998b). Rhetorically, this identity requires a specific standard of judgment: it requires that we "give up principled critique and develop a far more pluralistic and supple" approach to argument (40). Miller's specific edge in the conversation comes from his accusation that we in composition are deluded when we decry corporately-envisioned higher education reforms. Surely, he argues, we must know of the constraints surrounding emancipatory aims. If these constraints are known, we should not participate in the ritualized practice of "moral posturing in the academy's melodrama" (212).

Like White, Miller is not directly addressing the current reform debate, but he is making a clear argument about composition's rhetoric of professionalism. A pragmatic response focuses on how to work within bureaucratic terms and limits rather than invoking the transcendent; in Burke's pentadic terms, it subordinates the agent to the agency appropriate for the scene. Like White, Miller's argument employs a realist style to call for a specific kind of response: at least on the surface, this response must affect the detachment and defensibility of institutional policy. Like White, Miller imagines this bureaucratic rhetoric of professionalism as a means of enacting composition's values *even if* these means do not counter market-dominated public discourse about literacy education.

Like Miller, Donna Strickland (2011) understands the teaching of English as a bureaucratic or managerial practice. To be clear, Strickland is concerned with the material realities of composition teaching and administration that justify the "managerial" label and *not* with the practice of going public. But Strickland's attention to the material dimensions of composition also leads her to recommend how we in composition should make the case for our professional judgment. It is this dimension of Strickland's work that I draw out to connect her perspective with those summarized above. Strickland suggests we should forego invocations of democracy because such images deny the managerial realities of the field. In particular, she is suspicious of the romantic story that rescues "composition from its degraded and marginal status by repositioning the composition class as a unique site of democratic politics and political commitment" (6). Professional associations like CCCC, Strickland argues, use this rhetoric to produce disciplined teaching subjects who will submit to managerial control in the name of democratic access for students (56). Instead of denying the managerial, Strickland suggests, "we can embrace the role of manager, not because it is a good or because it is the only way to get things done. We can embrace it because it is ours and because it deserves much more attention if we are to truly work for the material benefit of administrators, teachers, and students alike" (122). Rhetorically, embracing managerialism entails a suspicion of our invocations of the transcendent, which Strickland reads as self-affirming rather than substantive (117). Rather than invoking the democratic, Strickland suggests, we would be better served by attending to the constraints of institutions and markets (118) and working as managers to achieve concrete benefits for us and others (122).

Like Miller, Strickland invokes the way the world is and names her judgment for going public pragmatism. The public of Strickland's argument is disciplinary and institutional rather than the public(s) of broader reform debate, but her definition of pragmatism has broader public implications. When speaking as administrators, Strickland suggests, we can acknowledge the managerial realities of our relationships rather than denying the managerial as a means of disciplining composition's labor force (114–19). Having recognized our managerial function, Strickland argues, "we can put our considerable intellectual abilities to work on the pragmatic, transformative tasks of tweaking, of deploying our work as 'performances requiring audience participation'" (121). These performances invite a give and take that is playfully critical of professional invocations of the democratic. With this turn, Strickland qualifies the realist style of scholars who advance a rhetoric of bureaucracy. She acknowledges the material realities that belie the conventional rhetorical performances of composition. In a way, Strickland aligns herself with Burke's comic critique: the self-critical manager of composition is one who acknowledges the conventionality of her rhetoric of professionalism. But Strickland also maintains her larger argument to the field: to attend to the material, we must check our use of the transcendent.

This rhetorical discipline suggests a way to rearticulate the idealist style of professionalism to the realist style of institutional and political reform. Rather than emphasizing composition's expansive values—democratic participation, collaboration, access to opportunity—bureaucratic judgment would enable us to make do with the available rhetorical resources to improve on the consequences of reform. But the scholars cited here attend mostly to the institutional contexts of composition. How might a managerial suspicion of the transcendent account for the public conversations surrounding emerging reforms like Complete College America? And how might a pragmatism of suspicion shape our efforts to go public outside our institutional boundaries? To explore these questions, I read bureaucratic innovation against the pragmatic aim it invokes, the process of defining and attending to consequences.[2]

BUREAUCRACY'S PRAGMATISM

Bureaucratic innovation takes up a line of inquiry famously prompted by philosopher William James (1907, 94): "what difference would it practically make to anyone if this notion rather than that notion were true?" James poses this question to suggest that stalemated debates may be reopened if participants step back from the struggle of advancing contending perspectives to reassess the consequences of these perspectives. Such an inquiry-seeking stance depends on an alternate standard of rhetorical judgment: rather than insisting on our preferred terms in debate, James suggests, we should seek out possibilities within the discourses at play in the situation. Adopting this pose can free us from our reliance on "fixed principles, closed systems, and pretended absolutes and origins" (97) and instead turn our attention "towards concreteness and adequacy, towards facts, towards action, and towards power." For composition's question of going public, James's provocation might be rephrased in the following ways: what does it matter if the terms for literacy education are democratic (as we professionals insist they must be) or standards- and market-based (as reformers insist they must be)? If the consequences of these discourses are complex and varied, can we attempt another rhetorical tactic in debate? Can we avoid reifying the realist-idealist style stalemate and possibly achieve favorable democratic consequences *despite* the dominance of standardizing and marketizing terms of reform? Here James's stance demonstrates the antiprofessionalism of pragmatic inquiry. Rather than maintaining a conventional appeal or rhetorical style, James pursues inquiry into consequences on the grounds that such consequences can better inform us how to proceed.

White, Miller, and Strickland, working from institutional contexts, take up James's goad to inquiry. Based on this inquiry, these scholars find opportunities within bureaucratic terms to improve on the negative material consequences associated with composition's conventional rhetoric of professionalism. Given these potential consequences, they suggest, we should not decry standardization or elevate our pluralism to the transcendent plane. Instead, we should innovate by testing appeals to bureaucracy for their capacity to secure material benefits for writing students, teachers, and administrators. In this view, rhetorically tending to the material is the *means* of delivering democratic ends. Within this scope, broader concerns of going public, such as the publics formed by the rhetoric of bureaucracy, can be set aside in the present context with the knowledge that institutional gains can support larger democratic aims.

Graff and Birkenstein, working in the public scope of contemporary reform, temper this judgment slightly. Whereas Miller calls for holding off on invoking transcendence, and Strickland acknowledges her suspicions of such invocations,

Graff and Birkenstein bring back the transcendent. Here, however, transcendence is no longer deployed as a reason to maintain conventional professional independence; instead, it is leveraged as a reason for us to innovate on our conventional rhetoric of professionalism. To serve democratic aims, we must subordinate our means to our ends. To go public, then, we need to adopt the means-ends wager of institutional bureaucracy. *This* is pragmatism for the public good, and while other pragmatisms may be well-intentioned, they fail to understand the relationship between rhetoric and context.

This judgment and accompanying rhetorical style is well represented in scholarly debates over the political and ethical scope of pragmatic inquiry. In his memorable "Truth and Toilets: Pragmatism and the Practices of Life," Stanley Fish (1998) argues that a pragmatic perspective on language commits us nothing more than learning to use the terms appropriate to a specific context. Echoing James, Fish terms pragmatism "an account of decision making and change that dispenses with decision procedures, hard and fast rules, and comprehensive theories, and emphasizes instead hunches, luck, creative opportunism, being in the right place at the right time with the right resources . . . but there is nothing you could do with it, for like the accounts it would dislodge, a pragmatist account has traction only in the context of the competition it seeks to win; in any other context, it is more or less useful depending on the purposes you are pursuing" (420). In Fish's view, such an account authorizes us to take on a rhetorical eclecticism. We may not like the dominant discourse, but "if we avail ourselves of it—with a lightness that will be bearable in that it does not penetrate to our being—it can be put in the service of what we do want" (421). Thus, Fish concludes, "if pragmatism is anything . . . it is an up-to-date version of rhetoric . . . that is the lesson that pragmatism teaches, that we live in a rhetorical world where arguments and evidence are always available, but always challengeable, and that the resources of that world are sufficient unto most days" (432). This doesn't mean anything goes, Fish adds, but rather that "anything that can be made to go goes."

It should come as little surprise, however, that this pragmatism is contested. As Robert Danisch (2007) argues, both rhetoric and pragmatism are committed to pluralism (142). Since the art of rhetoric is a key method of enacting pragmatist inquiry (14), the rhetorics we reappropriate matter. In this view, pragmatic rhetorical innovation is concerned not only with attending to consequences but also with the "ability to judge the best uses of knowledge, to predict the consequences of social action, and to act in the best interests of the community" (63). Certainly, this is what Fish and proponents of bureaucratic innovation claim to do. "The community" entails the profession and the students it serves; therefore, the appropriate means may be chosen to serve our broader ends. But Danisch's community is broader—it hearkens to "the great community" of Dewey's (1927, 174) *The Public*. This community is united not by institutional location, professional identity, or place but by its communicative practices—"methods of persuasion [that] allow for the participation of the public in the process of democratic decision-making, also known as deliberation" (Danisch 2007, 60). Rather than taking up rhetorics lightly, then, Danisch envisions the aim of pragmatic innovation along the lines Dewey (1927) articulates: "the improvement of the methods and conditions of debate, discussion, and persuasion" (208). From this perspective, Fish's rhetorical eclecticism takes up James's call to innovation but also narrows it.

The democratic groundings of phronesis are also the concern of philosopher Victor Kestenbaum (2002). He finds James's prompt useful in that it returns our attention to the relationship between our specific contexts and our rhetoric. But Kestenbaum also finds in this contextualism a tendency to narrow the scope of our rhetorical judgment and, by extension, the reach of the goods we seek. That is, Kestenbaum argues, "in its desire to keep ideal ends from straying too far from concrete means, to see how things are verified and worked out in experience, in short, in its desire to be practical, pragmatism foreshortens the power of what is in principle, as well as in fact, unrealizable" (15). The pragmatic way to square realities and ideals, Kestenbaum insists, is not to excise the transcendent. Rather, we should dwell with the sense of discontent between ideals and realities. When we take up this stance, we can recognize the role of the transcendent in our efforts at inquiry and innovation. Transcendent values like democracy highlight "moments when the ideal and transcendent are absorbed by the actual and the immanent, and moments when they resist such absorption. On these occasions, the ideal 'outruns' the actual, leaving our practices and habits, and pragmatism itself in a less certain state" (25–26). Here Kestenbaum is not saying that invoking the transcendent is a virtue unto itself. Rather, Kestenbaum argues that the experience of inquiry *requires* a conception of a transcendent end (26).

Rather than eclectically adopting commonplaces in context, then, Kestenbaum envisions pragmatic inquiry and innovation as the work of discovering the reasons we are dissatisfied with presently available terms for our values. This experience of discontent is important because it reminds us why we are seeking to participate in the melioration of problematic situations in the first place. As philosopher Ruth Anna Putnam (1998) argues, we take up this effort not because it offers us the lightness that Fish describes but because it satisfies our "passional grounds" (62)—the overlap of professional, personal, and public concerns. This, Putnam argues, is what underlies pragmatic inquiry and innovation—"we need to believe that there are other people with whom we share a common world and that our actions can make a difference to what that world will become" (68). So while we focus on "getting through" (2), in Koopman's terms, and we understand innovation as "those temporal and historical media in virtue of which we work through a situation from old to new" (11), we do this work with a larger aim—"reconstructing and reorienting the epistemic, ethical, and political realities in which we find ourselves flowing" (17). In this view, the larger aim of pragmatic rhetorical innovation is not merely using what we can but rather attempting what Dewey (1927) calls the improvement of the means of debate—enabling the kind of publics we want to inhabit.

To be sure, these counterstatements to Fish and to rhetorical eclecticism do not discount the pragmatism of bureaucratic innovation. Rather than saying what we usually say in our profession, proponents of bureaucracy reassess our rhetoric against what we really do. Like Dewey (1935), proponents of bureaucracy turn to our experiences to assess the capacity of contending perspectives to reflect our individual contexts (322). These contextual inquiries, in turn, enable us to draw broader conclusions about the capacity of shared terms for reflecting our worlds. Bureaucratic innovation enacts what Hephzibah Roskelly and Kate Ronald recognize as the central faith of pragmatic inquiry: "the more varied the sites of inquiry, and the greater the number of inquirers, the more useful the conclusions" (Roskelly and Ronald 1998, 90). By circulating accounts of our diverse experiences in various institutional settings, proponents of bureaucracy invite us to inquire into the adequacy of our conventional terms for reflecting our experiences.

Yet these bureaucratic innovations tend to focus on one kind of experience: institutional and political agents affirming composition professionals' judgment so long as that judgment is framed in bureaucratic terms. Based on these experiences, the material and the managerial are imagined as replacing the transcendent valence of idealist style. Within this perspective, there's little room for rhetoric as the discovery of alternate perspectives, nor is there room for the encompassing ambiguities of democratic possibility. In the institutional context of the scholarship cited here, such a bureaucratic scope of consequences may make sense. But for teachers, scholars, and administrators who seek to foster a broader set of public rhetorical experiences when going public, bureaucratic innovation offers less guidance: proponents of bureaucracy urge us to set aside our concerns with rhetoric as an experiential means of public formation and engagement so that we can advance professional goods. If we can advance professional goods, the argument goes, we can advance democracy.

In "A Progressive Case," Graff and Birkenstein (2008) echo this conclusion, forwarding a pragmatic standard of judgment that recognizes appeals to institutional standardization as a potentially *public* rhetoric of professionalism. They attenuate composition's emphasis on the enlarging rhetorical experience of professional appeals to pluralism and reclaim standardiza tion (both at the level of rhetoric and policy) as a means of democratization. In other words, Graff and Birkenstein affirm what White, Miller, and Strickland suggest—that material conse- quences form the means of the democratic. But with this means- ends wager, Graff and Birkenstein also reproduce the scope of the scholarly discussion: they assume the responsiveness of our publics to our bureaucratic appeals while setting aside the ques- tion of the rhetorical experiences fostered by bureaucratic inno- vation. What Graff and Birkenstein don't ask, in other words, is how fully the means-ends wager of institutional standardization extends to the public spheres of reform debate.

Should we wager that democratic access to opportunity can be increased by appeals to standardization rather than by appeals to the transcendent aims of pluralism? Roskelly and Ronald (1998) doubt such a question can be answered by pragmatic inquiry. Citing Cornel West (1989), they argue that "such ulti- mate agreement never comes" (91). But Roskelly and Ronald recognize in pragmatism "a regulative ideal and a hope that sustains rational adjudication and motivates scientific inquiry in the present" (91). In this light, our invocations of "pragmatism" should not affirm bureaucracy's public-professional wager so much as goad us to reopen inquiry into this wager. We should ask, then, again and again, and in as many contexts as possible with as many inquirers as possible, whether there is another way of going public.

While bureaucratic innovation takes up pragmatic aims, it also foreshortens inquiry on the grounds of an attenuated scope of rhetorical purposes for going public. Still, by attending to the material consequences and contexts of our work, proponents of bureaucratic innovation articulate a valuable pragmatic critique of our conventional rhetoric of professionalism. How, then, might this critique be extended for the theory and practice of going public? I find a model of this inquiry in Amy Wan's (2011)

"In the Name of Citizenship," which assesses the way we go public. By contending with Wan's critique of our rhetoric of professionalism, I suggest, we can adapt bureaucratic innovation for the contemporary scenes and purposes of reform debate.

ANOTHER PRAGMATISM

In an analysis of our disciplinary and public arguments about the aims of literacy education, Wan shares a concern with Graff and Birkenstein as well as White, Miller, and Strickland: all reassess the capacity of our terms to reflect the contexts of our work. Wan identifies citizenship as composition's key term for the public good of professionalism. Because this term allows us to claim that "successful writing instruction plays a key role in the preparation of good citizens" (28), we rely on it heavily, elevating it to the status of a "rote invocation" (46). But what Wan calls "the rhetorical function of citizenship" (29) is complex. The flexibility of the term allows us to link our professional judgment to a "capacious" (30) and "ambient" (29) sense of positive opportunity. At the same time, this "super term" (29) also encompasses conflicting perspectives on citizenship under the transcendent rubric of literacy-for-democracy. This rhetorical expansiveness allows professionals and others to "elide critical concerns about the access, impact, and exercise of citizenship" (29).

The danger of such elisions, Wan argues, is that appeals to citizenship can be reappropriated by those outside our profession. When Wan argues that "engaging citizenship as a classroom practice remains a murky undertaking with potential to undermine aspirations for the democratizing aspects of literacy" (30), she is not arguing in the abstract. She points to the Spellings Commission's claims to reconcile competing conceptions of literacy—individual achievement and equity (42)—as a caution to us in composition. When we "use citizenship and its rhetorical cachet as a way to imagine students as agents beyond the institution" (33), Wan argues, we broaden the potential range of public conceptions of literacy brought to bear on education reform debate. This broadening can allow reform groups to reappropriate equity for purposes we would consider antithetical to the value: see, for example, Complete College America's proposals to remove basic writing in the name of *increasing* access. With this caution, Wan is not addressing the question of how we might innovate on our defense of professionalism amid reform. But Wan is posing a challenge to our rhetoric of transcendence for going public. Unlike proponents of bureaucratic innovation, Wan's call is not to suspend the transcendent, nor is it to adopt the rhetoric of standardization and management as means to a democratic end. Instead, Wan urges us to inquire into the relationship of our rhetorical means to our democratic ends: "rather than make a simple call to action in name only, we need to deliberate on the habits of citizenship that are being cultivated through our actions . . . We should acknowledge the limitations of what citizenship can do for students, as well as the limitations put on students by the idea of citizenship. And we should create a space where our own citizen-making through the teaching of literacy is a more deliberate activity, one that enlivens the concept of citizenship by connecting classroom practices to other instances of citizenship production" (46). Here Wan suggests an alternate perspective on the exigency invoked by proponents of bureaucratic innovation. While these proponents note the disjunction between democratic possibilities and material realities in composition and advocate for suspending the rhetoric of the transcendent in favor of the managerial, Wan calls for an alternate practice. She calls for a focus on *acts*, the "everyday activities that may be mediated through habits and practices like the literate skills learned in classrooms and beyond" (45), and a shift of the scene of composition inquiry from the institutional sphere of bureaucracy to a multiplicity of scenes, including classrooms, publics, and workplaces. In this shift, Wan's move is not to write off an encompassing sense of purpose or elevate it uncritically. Instead, her innovation is to reread the "ambient" nature of citizenship against acts in specific contexts.

The purpose of this inquiry resonates with the concerns of Graff and Birkenstein as well as the others scholars cited above. How we construe literate acts of citizenship, Wan argues, shapes the material conditions of literacy education. After all, she argues, "gaining access to resources is what gives individuals the ability to enjoy these rights and to live as full citizens." Like Wan, then, the scholars discussed here recognize the limits of composition's rhetoric of professionalism and attempt to reconsider the relationship between our rhetorical means and our democratic ends. This reconsideration, however, tends to resolve quickly to the available resources of the context—namely, appeals to standardization as a means of securing material consequences. What we need instead, Wan suggests, is a rhetoric that attends to the full range of consequences across institutional-public boundaries. In an echo of the antiprofessionalism outlined in chapter 1, Wan calls for inquiry into literate practice that may affirm the transcendence of professional pluralism—our claimed public good—*or* that may suggest another set of terms. Rather than going public in order to maintain our conventional appeal, then, we can attend to acts of literate practice and potentially scale up from there. Yes, the transcendent aims of access, democracy, and citizenship might arise from such inquiry, but so might a common agency—the kinds of literate means necessary for different kinds of citizenship. In other words, the contextual inquiry of pragmatism might point toward professionalism as the means of democratization, or it might point toward standardization. We don't know.

What might Wan's inquiry mean for going public? Can its antiprofessionalism serve professionalism? I see an opportunity to extend bureaucratic innovation in the same way that Wan does citizenship: by focusing on student acts. This shift still allows us in composition the possibility of scaling up from acts to transcendent democratic possibilities, although not in the rote way that Wan argues is customary. Rather, by performing our inquiry into acts of teaching, learning, and assessment, we can ground our rhetorical judgment in concrete practices and highlight the experiential and material consequences of that judgment. By preserving the potential link between acts and purpose, we leave open the opportunity for our publics to connect professionalism to public goods.

I read Wan this way because her analysis of citizenship's flexibility anticipates the tactic of contemporary reform groups like
CCA. When Wan warns that our frequent invocations of citizenship enable corporate-political reformers to advance competing visions of literacy under the name of access (39), she
aptly describes the process through which CCA has advanced
its reforms. The stated aims of CCA are to improve democratic
access to opportunity for all students. But the means of doing
this tell another story. The CCA's "policy levers" are the familiar neoliberal tools: implementing performance based funding,
ending remediation, expanding course delivery methods, and
decreasing time to degree.[3] In my state, the Nevada System of
Higher Education (NSHE) began implementing these levers in
2012 through local "curriculum alignment" and "partnership
with K–12" (NSHE 2010). At my institution, "alignment" and
"partnership" meant that University of Nevada, Reno (UNR)
students could no longer register to take basic writing (English
098) as a part of their undergraduate education; they could
only take basic writing through the department of Continuing
Education so that UNR would record no more "remedial" numbers. In concert with UNR, the superintendent of the local
school district announced a pilot program to have high school
teachers in the district pre-teach 098 to UNR-bound students
identified as needing remediation.

With such initiatives being developed off the public stage and
implemented in a manner expressly designed to prevent our
participation, K–16 articulation reforms can seem inevitable.
"Access" may appear to fit seamlessly within proposals for the
marketization of expertise, and we in composition may reason-
ably conclude that there's little point in responding critically
to CCA. Better then, we might reason, to reappropriate efforts
like CCA at the institutional and program levels where we have
more influence and reform groups have less. We can go bureaucratic, in other words, to serve our democratic ends. But such
a pragmatic judgment forecloses on the potential for a broader
range of public rhetorical experiences amid reform. This judgment writes off the possibility that an alternate style of going

public can invite public participation and reopen the discussions closed by CCA's appropriation of access.

I glimpsed this possibility inadvertently when I showed CCA's materials to writing majors enrolled in a capstone-level professional writing class. I had introduced CCA's *Bridge to Nowhere* (Complete College America 2012) as an example of how advocacy groups frame their positions as service to public good, but after reading the first page of *Bridge*, my student Anthony wanted to engage with the claims of reform. He bristled at CCA's characterization of "remediation" as wasteful because, as he put it, "I took 098 here, and it allowed me to become a writing major." Although I had envisioned *Bridge* as a professional writing case study, Anthony's response suggested another purpose for composition teachers, scholars, and administrators to invite student inquiry into CCA: such inquiry is relevant to public participation in reform debate. For many students in Nevada and elsewhere, basic writing is a key experience. Students value it, it allows them to advance academically, and in retrospect, it can be recognized as a catalyst for personal transformation. But these sorts of classes are being eliminated in the name of cutting waste. This reform argument has an edge that students did not ignore: for groups like CCA, public investment in students like Anthony is "wasteful."

We already sense this edge, of course, and we respond by insisting that *all* students need our expert judgment to ensure access to opportunity. But such an argument tends to collapse into idealist style, a calcified appeal for preserving composition's professionalism against the neoliberalization of expertise. The kind of inquiry Wan envisions, however, suggests a way to innovate on our conventional approach to going public. Rather than immediately scaling up to citizenship, we can begin with our students' experiences with literacy development. My student Anthony, for example, started with basic writing courses, became an anthropology major, added a writing major, and in his capstone class with me, he researched a local nonprofit's grant writing materials, compared these materials to those of peer organizations, and developed genre and rhetorical guidelines for future nonprofit grant writers. In CCA's terms, Anthony moved from waste to value.

To the chagrin of groups like CCA, however, this movement took five years and not four. Never mind during these five years, Anthony worked full time and volunteered as a teacher of native languages at a local urban reservation; five years is waste. When we attend to Anthony's experience, however, we can see the crucial role of time: his rhetorical and stylistic maturity emerged through repeated opportunities for growth at multiple levels. I'm guessing that many of us have students like Anthony who may have taken years off after high school, attended a community college, perhaps transferred to a four-year college or university, and then entered our writing courses. When I meet students like Anthony in their fifth or sixth years, they are often as well as or even better prepared than younger students who moved through college in four years. Given what he'd earned over time, Anthony felt what many of us probably feel when we read the CCA's materials: anger at the way reformers invoke "waste" to discount student potential for growth over time. In composition, we know that groups like CCA invoke "remediation" because it is at the level of the broad, political-economic abstractions of "waste" that reformers can earn political support for disinvestment in public education. For Anthony, however, waste is personal. It's his life they're talking about.

If Anthony felt outrage after a few minutes of class discussion, I believe other students can also explore how their experiences are selected, reflected, and deflected in CCA's public messaging. Here, I envision going public as inviting our students to assess CCA's realist style against their experiences. Accounts of assessments like Anthony's, in turn, can be circulated to sponsor student conversations elsewhere about disinvestment-themed reforms like CCA. Anthony's response demonstrates that writing instruction over time matters not just because experts endorse such an approach or even because such instruction supports "access"; rather, Anthony's response shows how basic writing responds to public experience with literacy. To perform our inquiry into reform with our students, I argue, is to invite students to participate in their own inquiry, which can sponsor further public assessment of reform's proposals for teaching and learning. In a departure from our conventional rhetoric of professionalism, such a response to reform would assert not only the necessity of the professional agent to enact the agency of basic writing expertise. As CCA's argument demonstrates, an appeal to the agency of basic writing is being reappropriated to be delivered via standardization and marketization. Instead, our approach would focus public attention on the grounds of the contextual judgments we make.

Of course, reformers' response to these grounds is to dismiss them. In public messaging, CCA speaks only of changing remediation *as a system*. Such a response has been effective at staving off our appeals to expert contextualism as democractic representation. But reformers' totalizing argument has not yet faced the circulation of public inquiry into experiences like Anthony's. The aim of an alternate realist style is to enable our publics to reassess the capacity of contemporary reforms to respond to their experiences with writing. While an alternate realist response does not assert the superiority of professionalism over neoliberalism, it does suggest a way to sponsor broader public inquiry into and critique of otherwise off-stage policy developments like CCA.

My call here, then, is for an innovation on going public that recognizes the potential value of transcendence, but as we reach it through rhetorical experiences of inquiry. Such an innovation would recognize our need to have this experience as professionals—to determine how to go public. And such a style would recognize our publics' need for this rhetorical experience so that they can break up the market-professionalism stalemate through contextual inquiry. Definitions of the public goods served by literacy education are certainly muddied in the current moment, and the competing definitions advanced by professionals and reformers are stalemated, but my student Anthony's experience suggests that our innovation on going public needs to do more than narrow the grounds of our judgment. Instead, I argue, our innovation needs to scale down to scale up to the broader democratic aims of professional judgment.

GOING PUBLIC IN THE ERA OF JUST-IN-TIME SUPPORT (JIT)

It is impossible to make this argument, however, without acknowledging that antiprofessionalism is a hard sell when we face clear challenges to our professionalism. Instead of connecting basic writing to the undergraduate curriculum, groups like CCA call for "just-in-time support" (JIT). In place of "remedial" courses as prerequisites to credit-bearing college courses, CCA proposes a "co-requisite" model in which more students are "mainstreamed" into college-level gateway courses (Complete College America 2011, 15) and offered mandatory JIT support. CCA never defines what this support might look like except that it should come from writing and tutoring centers rather than classes. Why are such forms of support preferable to basic writing courses? CCA's terms offer a clue: in business management, the field from which JIT is drawn, JIT philosophy aims to simplify manufacturing processes and cut waste. In a representative definition, Cambridge University's Management Technology Policy Program (Cambridge University Institute for Manufacturing 2015) names the goals of JIT as "low inventory," "low waste," "high quality production," and "high customer responsiveness." In the instructional context, "low inventory" suggests fewer people on instructional staff. Less "waste" would imply fewer full-time-equivalent instructors dedicated to "remediation." And lower staffing overhead, presumably, would imply more "quality" and "responsiveness" to students: without set course schedules, we can support students' needs more flexibly. In the contemporary reform context, these goals are familiar. JIT seeks to speed students' paths to graduation by shifting basic writing from classes to support settings and opening those support settings to a marketplace of service providers. It envisions market competition and consumer choice improving the delivery of educational services, and this improved delivery improving outcomes.

While composition teachers, scholars, and administrators have not yet responded directly to CCA, we have already begun fashioning an answer to JIT philosophy. Despite JIT's resonance with neoliberal deprofessionalization, some writing centers and professionally-led software developers have begun embracing JIT as a "tool" for improving writing instruction. In a post to *Another Word*, the University of Wisconsin–Madison's Writing Center blog, David Charbonneau (2012) describes JIT as an integral part of his approach to directing a writing center at Mt. San Antonio College, the largest single-campus community college in California. For Charbonneau, "'developmental writing' in the community college means something different than it does in most four-year contexts." That is, composition instructors at community colleges cannot assume students have developed the reading comprehension skills needed to undertake the work envisioned in our scholarship. Instead of worrying about teaching "the whole writer" or "inventing the university," Charbonneau suggests, the community college instructor has more pressing needs—teaching "foundations" like "'the five paragraph essay,' the structure of a paragraph, identification and correction of fragments and run-ons, and basic summarizing." Moreover, Charbonneau insists, we must teach students foundations quickly and under the pressure of budget cuts. Charbonneau's response to these constraints is to adopt Directed Learning Activities (DLAs) which require students to complete online exercises before meeting with writing center consultants. For Charbonneau, this arrangement represents a step forward: DLAs are cost effective, they address gaps in students' knowledge, and offer us "another potential tool in our kit." In a reflection on his own learning process, Charbonneau insists that this tool "has helped [him] to learn that sometimes in learning to address 'the whole writer,' we need to build up from discrete parts that make up that whole."

Charbonneau's self-reflection offers an implicit goad to writing professionals as a whole: when our institutions demand skills, we would do well to reappropriate the language and delivery practices endorsed by contemporary reform. In line with the bureaucratic innovation discussed above, Charbonneau wagers that an appeal to standardization can advance the democratic aims of composition. What Charbonneau doesn't discuss in this endorsement, however, are the possible consequences of adopting "tools" for teaching "discrete parts." The DLAs listed on Mt. San Antonio's Writing Center site offer a clue to these consequences. These modules emphasize the twenty most common errors usually featured in composition handbooks. Charbonneau claims that the DLAs allow writing center consultants to address sentence-level issues in the context of students' writing, but the site stipulates that students are required to address these issues *before* talking with a consultant about their writing. This approach illustrates one of the potential consequences of creating "tools" in the era of JIT. When our professional judgment can be abstracted and mechanized for the sake of efficiency, our institutions can separate teachers and teaching, agents and agency. In this environment, it becomes possible to build a marketplace of expertise where entrepreneurial developers of exercises and writing content can displace the homegrown and contextual materials created by professionals. For administrators seeking to cut costs, DLAs may suggest a way for colleges and universities to do the work of Writing Centers *without having a Writing Center.*

Such framing matters especially now that entrepreneurs like WriteLab are positioning themselves as writing service providers to institutions. In December 2015, WriteLab representatives gave a demonstration of their software at my campus. I was intrigued by WriteLab's (2016) claim to "analyze students' prose to deliver customized feedback—observations, compliments, and suggestions." Such an approach, WriteLab claims, "helps students in-process become more effective writers." This sounds very much like the aim of JIT, in which automated responses preserve cost-effectiveness while approximating teachers' contextual judgment. In the terms of this chapter, WriteLab forwards bureaucracy as a means of delivering access to opportunity. But when I logged into WriteLab's site, I found it offering little of the contextual judgment that we in composition associate with the teaching of writing. Rather than engaging the student in a conversation about the assignment or the status of the draft—is this writing to learn? writing to communicate?—WriteLab analyzes the textual features it associates with pre-defined qualities of writing: Clarity, Logic, Emphasis, Coherence, Cohesion, Concision, Elegance. Certainly, these are important qualities. But against its promotional claims, WriteLab appears to offer an interactive version of a first-year writing handbook, not contextual judgment.

WriteLab may very well help institutions teach more writing in their classes. But my question here is not about quantity; it's about quality, and these images of the acts of teaching and responding are impoverished. As in the redirection of JIT on display in the Mt. St. Antonio Writing Center, WriteLab's reappropriation of the tools of reform has experiential consequences. It retreats from composition professionals' unique strength, which is that we read student writing and ask questions *before* deploying abstractable algorithms. *This* is what we have to offer our publics, and I believe it is what our publics can appreciate when we invite their inquiry into acts of teaching. At the risk of adopting a realist style of my own in the contemporary political economy, I argue that we can't offer "tools" like WriteLab unless we want them to be used in the marketplace of competing service providers. We can't offer up such "tools" unless we want to enable our institutions to disinvest in our teaching.

Strong words, I know. But WriteLab trades on its developers' professional expertise to stave off the critique that the company's aims are merely entrepreneurial. If professionalism is what separates WriteLab from Pearson or other service providers in a marketplace of expertise, it is fair to ask WriteLab what is professional about its judgment. One of WriteLab's most prominent ambassadors offers an answer to this question. Just before WriteLab representatives came to my campus, I received a WriteLab promotional email from Les Perelman. I was interested to learn how Perelman saw himself in relation to WriteLab since he has, in his own words, "become a frequent critic of automated essay scoring and most computer applications intended for writing classrooms." Over the last six months, Perelman (2015) explains, he's gotten involved with WriteLab, which features "two eminent compositionists," Donald McQuade, a former chair of CCCC, and Richard Sterling, a former director of the National Writing Project. This joining of professional expertise and "tools" led to something Perelman didn't expect: a "student-centered" technology for writing.

Like me, Perelman expected to find WriteLab giving high scores to gibberish like other assessment service providers (ETS, Pearson, Turnitin). But instead he found that WriteLab doesn't score essays. *This* as the centerpiece of Perelman's argument surprised me. I agree it's better to have machines giving feedback instead of scoring student writing, but feedback also requires judgment. To me, then, it doesn't matter that the program "returns authority to the student" to enact or ignore WriteLab's feedback. (What is the quality of this feedback?) Nor is it much of a selling point that "WriteLab learns from and adapts to the writer's preferences," unless this means that WriteLab wants to learn what kind of feedback the student is seeking at a certain point on her draft. (As far as I can tell, it doesn't.) By the time I got to the end of Perelman's email, I felt baited and switched. I wanted to believe in WriteLab's "for teachers, by teachers" appeal. But instead I found a familiar line of argument, an appeal to the way the world is. The dramatic peroration of Perelman's email reminds us that "technology is a part of our lives and a part of our writing. Word processors and spell checkers are integral to our writing habits. A tool that uses machine learning to analyze writing is inevitable, and if the composition community doesn't build it correctly, others will build it badly."

Here I cannot be alone in hearing echoes of the realist style described in this book: Richard Miller exhorting us to learn to be good bureaucrats; Ed White urging us to get used to the language of bureaucracy; and Linda Adler-Kassner and Peggy O'Neill insisting that, like it or not, we need to temper our public critiques of reform's assessments to make appreciable change (see chapter 3). I heard, in other words, an appeal to a specific kind of pragmatism about going public. To go public in this moment means making use of the available means, getting through, reappropriating and redirecting larger trends that encompass us. We can do it ourselves or have it done unto us. What I didn't hear, however, was a discussion of the broader consequences I've outlined in this book and in this chapter in particular. Nor did I get a sense of the public good of companies like WriteLab claiming to offer tools in a market of third-party service providers. Does WriteLab envision itself contributing to CCA's good markets for good democracy? Can consumer choice deliver public goods more fully than professional perspectives on instruction? These questions are set aside through WriteLab's entrepreneurial premise, which discourages us from quibbling with its claims about "customizable" feedback. Instead, WriteLab encourages us, be grateful that this program is dealing *just* with sentence and paragraph level concerns. But those concerns, while more modest than machine scoring's usual claims to assess meaning, are still significant in the larger context: these are machine-runnable "tools" that enable and accelerate the neoliberalization of expertise.

In 2016, I heard that Perelman disassociated himself with WriteLab because he saw it reducing the act of responding and teaching more broadly to the norms of contemporary reform: standardization, routinization, and marketization. Among these dominant mechanisms, apparently, the bureaucratic wager was no longer worth making. As the logic of JIT comes more fully into view, we will need to do something similar—re-evaluate both our conventional defenses of professionalism and our innovations. Our response to JIT is worth considering critically because as professionals, we have an interest in limiting the higher education marketplace for writing expertise. My argument here, however, is not just that we should oppose JIT on the grounds that it casualizes academic labor and decreases the value of our expertise. Rather, I am urging us to raise questions about JIT on the grounds that it fails to engage with what we value—the acts of professional response to writing. Each of the responses to JIT described here offer composition little ground on which to counter reforms like CCA. Instead of performing our inquiry into acts of teaching and inviting public inquiry that can disclose the grounds of professional judgment, these responses are turning away from the contingency of our judgment. In the neoliberal moment, this contingency can look like weakness, but I argue that it is our public strength, the one thing that JIT cannot displace.

This is the challenge of pragmatic innovation when going public. An attention to consequences enables us to re-evaluate our rhetoric of professionalism. But this same attention can crop out our experience as teachers, scholars, and administrators seeking to go public. When we argue that we have been wise amid constraints—that we have been pragmatic—we tend to congratulate ourselves for having saved ourselves and our profession the time and energy of inquiry. But in this move, we tend to forget the value of our inquiry experience. In "The Moral Struggle or the Realizing of Ideals," Dewey (1969) puts this forgetting in stark terms. He names the challenge of pragmatist inquiry to be "surrender," but not the surrender of ideals to constraints. Rather, Dewey argues, the challenge is to "surrender the actual experienced good for a possible ideal good" (372). This stance offers terms for assessing the pragmatism of a bureaucratic rhetoric. What surrender does it ask of us—the experienced good of institutional power or the possible ideal good of public engagement? This argument is not stated openly, but in its effort to fashion rhetorical ends-in-view under constraints, proponents of bureaucratic innovation discount the ideal good as a source of aspirations for change. Moreover, in disciplining our public arguments, a bureaucratic rhetoric of professionalism denies our publics potential opportunities to experience their own discontent between the dominant terms of reform (competitiveness, standardization) and their own experiences of the transcendent, which may disclose many other key terms—not just the global competitive scene but also local scenes, multiple agencies of writing, a range of agents, and a host of purposes. In its effort to reappropriate a materialist rhetoric of management, a bureaucratic rhetoric of professionalism also limits the potential of pragmatic inquiry to support composition's public aims.

I opened this chapter by defining bureaucracy as an attempt to fashion solutions using "the resources already furnished in that situation" (Koopman 2009). My analysis suggests that bureaucratic innovation only partly accounts for the limits of managerialism as a rhetoric of public engagement. If it did, proponents of bureaucracy would likely recognize the experiential consequences of going public and, in particular, the role of the transcendent in pragmatic inquiry. Attention to these consequences suggest a broader role for our contextual judgment in going public and for inviting public participation in assessing professional judgment. Such a focus on the experiential and the transcendent may well undermine composition's managerial aspirations, but this focus may also advance our aims to develop a public rhetoric of professionalism in an era of reform. In the following chapter, I explore an effort in composition to do just this. Reframing resituates professionalism within a transcendent sense of possibility—a democratic togetherness served by shared professional judgment—all while negotiating the constraints of reform discourse.

NOTES

1. For example, circa 2010 the National Governors Association encouraged sympathetic governors to sign onto Complete College America. From there, chancellors of state systems of higher education were tasked with implementing CCA's policy levers. As I discuss later in this chapter, the standardization envisioned by CCA did not seek professional contributions; instead, it sought to work against them.

2. Robert Danisch (2007) calls a concern with consequences the central tenet of pragmatism (54).

3. For example, this Completion Academy in Missouri is typical: http://dhe .mo.gov/mo-completion-academy.php.

Chapter 3

REFRAMING, PROPHETIC PRAGMATISM, AND ARTFUL CRITIQUE

Pointing out what is wrong does not provide anyone a hand-hold for acting upon what is right—in other words, it doesn't provide the foundation for a proactive strategy that can reframe issues important to us. Instead, it puts us only in a reactive mode—and reaction, in the long run, only perpetu-ates the issues being critiqued in the first instance.
—Linda Adler-Kassner and Peggy O'Neill,
Reframing Writing Assessment (2010, 167)

In this forceful passage, Adler-Kassner and O'Neill forward a stan-dard of rhetorical wisdom for going public. We may *want* to dis-miss quantitative measures of student learning and reassert the primacy of our qualitative perspectives for improving literacy edu-cation (39). But in the contemporary K–16 reform scene, we ben-efit little by situating ourselves in opposition to those who work in the quantitative. Associating opposition with a refusal to engage, Adler-Kassner and O'Neill warn that "if we withdraw, get angry, or don't even enter these more public discussions, then we aren't able to have any influence at all, and it is unlikely that our val-ues and perspectives will be represented" (155). For the authors, these potential consequences require a re-evaluation of our rhe-torical judgment for going public. We can say what's wrong with the assessments promoted by reform, but we must remember what is at stake: "if we don't get involved and try to make the sys-tem better," we will be "abrogating our responsibilities as profes-sionals" (165). If going public is going to make a difference, in other words, we must reconsider our conventional style.

DOI: 10.7330/9781607326540.c003

As readers of this book may recall, however, this standard of judgment was soon challenged. Not long after the Common Core entered the implementation phase (2011–12), the K–12 assessment consortia of PAARC (Partnership for Assessment of Readiness for Colleges and Careers) and Smarter Balanced announced their plans to use a combination of human- and machine-scoring to evaluate students' responses to the Common Core's written performance tasks. In response to these plans, a group of writing teachers, scholars, and administrators circulated the Human Readers (HR) petition, which asserted that machines cannot "measure the essentials of effective written communication: accuracy, reasoning, adequacy of evidence, good sense, ethical stance, convincing argument, meaningful organization, clarity, and veracity, among others" (Human Readers 2015). Machine scoring can't assess these qualities of writing, HR argued, because its methodology is "trivial," "reductive," "inaccurate," "undiagnostic," "unfair," and "secretive." To support authentic writing and make good judgment on behalf of the public, HR insisted, we need human readers.

Such an appeal envisions a specific form of rhetorical wisdom. HR does not contain its critiques to the disciplinary-professional sphere; instead, its petition attempts to expand public concern with reform. It forwards machine scoring as a shared problem, a failure of PAARC and Smarter Balanced to account for students', parents', and administrators' experiences with writing. From this perspective, there is only one way to address this public problem, and that is to restore our professional roles as readers in assessment. When our professional critiques have been ignored, we have no choice but to open the question of assessment to public debate. Then, perhaps, we can sponsor critical public perspectives on assessment and earn, once again, our rightful standing as representatives of public values. In this light, to name the problems of reform is to point toward their necessary solutions.

This standoff between reframing and critique poses a question. What about critique misunderstands the political economy of contemporary reform? Why *does* critique limit us as professionals and by extension, hurt our capacity to represent our publics? I explored similar questions in chapter 2 by assessing the rhetoric of bureaucracy as an innovation on going public. That innovation taps into the central effort of pragmatism —attending to and improving on the consequences of human action. In this chapter, I assess reframing as a closely related innovation. Reframing enacts another key pragmatic effort, the melioration of problematic situations. Reframing's melioration is to improve on the consequences of going public by reopening inquiry into our conventional rhetorical practice. Is professional critique of reform adequate to improving teaching, learning, and assessment in the ways that composition values? For proponents of reframing, it is not. Rather than *publicly* critiquing corporate-political efforts to measure college readiness and outcomes, then, we should contain our critiques to our professional and disciplinary spheres. In public, we should *redirect* calls for reform to reflect composition's values (Adler-Kassner 2008; Adler-Kassner and Harrington 2010; Adler-Kassner and O'Neill 2010). Such tactical political action, Adler-Kassner insists, would not only acknowledge our marginalized position in the politics of reform (172) but also enact the "prophetic pragmatism" of Cornel West (1989). West envisions critics "transform[ing] linguistic, social, cultural, and political traditions for the purposes of increasing the scope of individual development and democratic operations" (230); proponents of reframing suggest that we can work toward such aims by seeking opportunities to redirect and expand reform terms like "college- and career-readiness."

Like Graff and Birkenstein's bureaucratic innovation, reframing responds to contemporary reform while also engaging with composition's ongoing scholarly discussion. Whereas Graff and Birkenstein largely echo disciplinary calls for a bureaucratic rhetoric, however, proponents of reframing are concerned with *reconciling* the disciplinary stalemate between managerial and critical perspectives. The managerial perspective is expressed most forcefully by Richard Miller (1998a), who calls on teachers, scholars, and administrators to recognize the profound constraints under which they work (5). If we recognize these realities, Miller insists, we must "give up principled critique and develop a far more pluralistic and supple" approach to argument about teaching and administration (40). Like the rhetorical eclecticism discussed in chapter 2, Miller's "supple" rhetorical judgment would seek out potential in the reappropriation and redirection of the key terms of institutional life. A critical perspective on going public, meanwhile, is expressed most forcefully by Marc Bousquet (2003), who questions calls for a pragmatism that works within rather than challenges logics of management (13). For Bousquet, scholar-administrators' invocations of pragmatism tend to "[conceal their] own market idealism underneath a rhetoric of exclusive purchase on reality" (25). For scholars advancing a critical perspective, the realist style of reform forwards not only a reductive vision of writing but also an impoverished model of the public sphere in which global competition obviates the need for public or professional participation in shaping educational policy. In this view, redirecting such a model of public representation, even for the purposes of expanding it, undermines composition's commitment to democratic values.

Proponents of reframing enter this standoff from a particular angle. By invoking prophetic pragmatism, these scholars reposition the management of composition's public discourse on a democratic horizon. In this line of thinking, redirecting reform's realist style enables teachers, scholars, and administrators to achieve the critical aim of improving public discourse about writing but without the problematic dimensions of public critique. Thus, proponents of reframing suggest, we in composition are better off moving beyond the convention of denouncing reform and the realist style that enables it. Instead of relying on critique for going public, we need to develop a public rhetoric of professionalism that works tactically within and potentially beyond realist style. In this light, pragmatism means redirecting market-framed discourse to serve democratic aims.

Such claims to pragmatic wisdom are hard to assess amid the crush of reform. Graff and Birkenstein's appeal to pragmatic inquiry, for example, is overshadowed by the seeming ease of

their embrace of standardization. Their call for outsider innovation sounds like a too-tough discounting of composition's
insider values. Reframing's appeal to pragmatism engages more
fully with insider values, yet its call for discipline, and particularly
professional discipline toward reforms couched in realist style, is
easy to read as an instance of what Kenneth Burke (1984a) calls
euphemism (166). What grounds reframing's wisdom of the
world and particularly of consequences unseen? What makes its
proponents certain that public critique is not worth the trouble?
And what if proponents of reframing are wrong, and by redirecting, we further advance the terms of reform in debate?

In this chapter, I explore how we in composition might engage
with the wisdom of redirection. What is a response that neither
affirms the claimed state of the world, in which public critique is
futile, nor rejects it, by insisting that critique is our professional
duty? One productive line of inquiry, I argue, is to read the pragmatism invoked against the pragmatism enacted. That is, how
does West's prophetic pragmatism envision the potentials and
limitations of critique? And what values, such as policy change
and other outcomes, are implicit in West's thinking on critique?
I take up this approach and argue that the pragmatism invoked
by proponents of reframing does more than affirm the wisdom
of redirection and the futility of critique. Instead, this pragmatism falls on the bias of the redirection/critique split, affirming
reframing's aims while also qualifying its suppression of critique
as a public response to realist style. Through an engagement
with perspectives from classical and contemporary pragmatism,
I seek to expand reframing as a response to composition's disciplinary dialectic and to the evolving scene of contemporary
reform. I find the pragmatic tradition providing such an enlarging vision by goading composition not only toward the redirection or denunciation of reform but also toward what John Dewey
(1935) calls an "artful" critique—a means of sponsoring local
public inquiry into and critique of the dominant direction of
reform. I forward artfulness as a means of reorienting teachers,
scholars, and professional associations toward public engagement as a means of going public. To illustrate the potential for

such engagement, I sketch out one way we might invite critical public inquiry into a central feature of contemporary reform, the machine scoring of writing. But I also attempt to qualify the potential of this form of engagement amid the profound constraints of the present: a Trump administration; a DeVos-led Department of Education; and Republican control in the House, the Senate, and a majority of governors' offices.

REFRAMING AND THE PROBLEM OF CRITIQUE

The practice of reframing proceeds from a central principle, a belief in teachers' and students' capacities for growth and improvement (Adler-Kassner 2008, 1). Proponents of reframing situate this belief in the philosophically pragmatic tradition, linking educational capacity building with John Dewey's efforts to develop critical public intelligence for solving shared problems (41). The practice of reframing aligns the critical efforts of the philosophically pragmatic tradition to outcome-oriented action strategies (Adler-Kassner and Harrington 2010, 93) that can be enacted in educational policy contexts from the institutional (88) to the national (O'Neill et al. 2012). The goal of such policy action is to advance composition's values of contextual pluralism amid reform.

At the heart of this practice is a standard of professional rhetorical judgment. To enact reframing, proponents argue, composition teachers, scholars, administrators, and professional associations must be strategic. With public discourse about literacy education dominated by appeals to standardization for global competitiveness, going public cannot simply dismiss the assessments forwarded by reform. This is not to say that reframing eschews critique wholesale: as Adler-Kassner and O'Neill (2010) make clear, *theoretical* critiques of reform are "an important first step" in situating "the assessments and the issues associated with them within our disciplinary expertise" (166–67). But critique does not allow us "to participate fully in discussions about large-scale assessment currently dominating the educational policy literature and popular discussions about education" (166). To engage these discussions, Adler-Kassner and O'Neill argue, we may build on terms already at play in reform-keyed assessments, including validity (75), reliability (79), and cross-institutional comparability (176).[1] Although these terms may at times seem to belong to the lexicon of contemporary reform, Adler-Kassner and O'Neill emphasize the neglected dimensions of these terms. We may be able to draw out these dimensions through give-and-take with those outside our profession (155). If we enter these dialogues, we can begin to tell a new "story of us" (88), a story that can help "stakeholders—whether colleagues in the program or department, campus administrators, community members, parents, or legislators—understand what it means to engage in *valid, reliable, and discipline-appropriate assessment that is used to improve teaching and learning*" (144; emphasis in original).

To be sure, Adler-Kassner and O'Neill's vision of reframing's possibilities is qualified. The authors acknowledge that reframing the key *terms* of reform doesn't dismantle the dominant *frame* of reform (177). Moreover, the authors admit that in the contemporary moment, reforms sometimes move so quickly that we may have few or no opportunities to participate in the processes of reframing described (158). But proponents of reframing nonetheless maintain that we are better off seeking to expand the stated values of assessment through dialogue with those who advance views unlike our own (35). This rhetorical judgment is preferable to critique because it appears to afford us more opportunities to further our central value as professionals: ensuring that contexts for assessment meaningfully reflect the rhetorical situations of writing (68–70). At stake, then, is the democratic function of our professionalism: reframing allows us to represent the literacy experiences of our diverse publics at a time when many reforms invoke manufacturing logics that would pre-define the inputs and outputs of teaching and learning (148). Rather than reject these logics, we have a responsibility to enlarge them through rhetorical inquiry and action. Quoting communication scholar James Carey, Adler-Kassner and O'Neill align this responsibility with the vision of public professionalism elaborated in Dewey's (1927) *The Public and Its Problems.* Changing stories about assessment can be understood as an "'effort to engage the public, not merely inform it, [to] . . . participate in, and not remain detached from, efforts to improve the quality of public discourse [and] understand . . . democracy as a way of life and not merely as a form of government'" (102).

We must do more than critique, then, because we cannot abandon our democratic professional errand. While Adler-Kassner and O'Neill decline to judge the "tradeoffs and short- and long-term gains" of reframing for "anyone but ourselves and our programs," (99), they nevertheless forward a broad conclusion on going public. If critique represents a refusal to engage debate, affirming critique is the "worst thing" we can do: it means "shirk[ing] our responsibilities" as literacy educators (178). The best thing we can do under the circumstances, then, is to manage critique. We should keep it theoretical and disciplinary, and for going public, we should channel our disapproval. Instead of asking how we can end the dominant frames for reform, we should ask how we can redirect them to reflect composition's values (Adler-Kassner and Harrington 2010, 94).

To underwrite this rhetorical judgment, scholars of reframing invoke the pragmatism of Saul Alinsky (Adler-Kassner and Harrington 2010, 87) and Dewey (Adler-Kassner 2008, 40) but locate themselves most clearly in Cornel West's "prophetic pragmatism." West's pragmatism, Adler-Kassner argues, reflects a "faith in/advocacy for the power of individuals to make a difference and improve democracy, balanced with acknowledgement that both these efforts and democracy is situated in and shot through with difference in power" (172). To make a difference, however, depends on a specific critical judgment. West argues that critics must "think genealogically about specific practices in light of the best available social theories, cultural critiques, and historiographic insights and to act politically to achieve certain moral consequences in light of effective strategies and tactics" (209). Scholars of reframing interpret this call to mean that compositionists must recognize that public critique cannot deliver the consequences they desire. Instead, we must approach reform tactically, redirecting K–16 articulation to strengthen rather than undermine our professional judgment.

By situating their judgment in the philosophically pragmatic tradition, scholars of reframing make both a disciplinary and a broader democratic claim. The disciplinary claim is that a critique of critique should not be understood as the managerial pragmatism Bousquet (2003) terms a rhetoric of "pleasing the prince" (12). Rather, scholars of reframing assert, such discipline should be understood as an invitation to compositionists to develop a standard of rhetorical judgment adequate to the constraints of going public. The democratic claim envisions a professionalism enabled by this rhetorical judgment. Reframing, these scholars suggest, can both defend our standing to shape policy amid reform *and* increase public engagement in questions of teaching, learning, and assessment (Adler-Kassner 2008, 82). From this perspective, message management can serve the democratic without the problematic dimensions of public critique.

The 2011 *Framework for Success in Postsecondary Writing* (The Council of Writing Program Administrators, The National Council of Teachers of English, and The National Writing Project 2012) demonstrates reframing as rhetorical tactic for going public. As O'Neill, Adler-Kassner, Cathy Fleischer, and Anne-Marie Hall explain in their introduction to the 2012 *College English* Symposium (O'Neill et al. 2012), the *Framework* is an attempt to address the exclusion of literacy educators' voices in public discussions of "college- and career-readiness" (520). The *Framework's* point of entry is the commonplace of public discussion: the competitive world invoked by the Common Core Standards Initiative and the attendant policy exigency (all students "career- and college-ready"). Rather than critique readiness, the *Framework* attempts to work within the limits established by the dominant discourse of reform: to be college ready, students need habits of mind developed through experiences with instructors in context. Thus, the *Framework* "describes the rhetorical and twenty-first century skills as well as habits of mind and experiences that are critical for college success" (525). If students have these habits of mind and experiences, they "will be well positioned to meet the writing challenges in the full spectrum of academic courses and later in their careers" (526). Again, the *Framework* "insinuates" (Farmer 2013, 148) literacy educators into the discussion, subtly shifting positioning professionalism as the *means* of reform, thus rearticulating reform's "readiness" and composition's contextual pluralism.

The *Framework* itself does not discipline composition's response to reform, but the document illustrates the explicit arguments made in the reframing scholarship: as professionals, we should respond to the threat of neoliberal displacement not through denunciation but through cooperation. To develop the habits of mind essential to success, students need the experiences that only we can provide in our writing courses. That way, at least, we can redirect reform to advance our values. That is, to advance composition's values is to declare ourselves a provider of expertise in the contemporary policy marketplace. But not all composition teachers, scholars, and administrators accept this standard of judgment. In her response to the *Framework*, for example, Christine Hansen (2012) rejects reframing as a rhetoric of professionalism for composition. Despite the rhetorical constraints around literacy educators K–16, Hansen insists that "we must reassert the importance of teachers' judgment in education. The huge state testing apparatuses that want to measure 'readiness' or 'competence' and the private industries that want to sell courses and tests, asserting the 'equivalence' of their products with our college courses, have usurped the role our society once allowed teachers to play: that of professionals whose judgment matters, whether in designing curriculum or assessing students" (542). Here Hansen does not attempt to mask her aims of responding to reform. The scare quotes around the key terms of reform (readiness, competence, equivalence), as well as the exploitation of devil terms (huge testing apparatuses, private industries, courses and tests for sale, usurping) make clear that she believes our professional discourse offers far more adequate terms than those forwarded by reform.

In the same Symposium, Judith Summerfield and Philip Anderson express a similar dissatisfaction with the *Framework's* response to reform (Summerfield and Anderson 2012). They want a framework that says what it wants in its own language rather than trying to reframe reform. In composition, Summerfield and Anderson argue, "we need a larger vision of literacy, a humanistic vision for educating our students that recognizes our students' capabilities, and one in which our 'framework' for practice makes our theories, and even ideology, explicit . . . We want to make explicit the underlying psychological, linguistic, cultural, philosophical, and pedagogical constructs. We think that the current trend toward 'commonsense' categories and academic formalism (now irretrievably transformed by and intertwined with social efficiency, that is, with managing behavior and 'preparing' students for vocations) is damaging to a half-century (at the least) of enlightened classroom study and socio-psycholinguistic research" (546–47). Here, especially in the scare quotes, is an explicit call to go public not through the discourse of reform but through the discourse of our profession(s). For Summerfield and Anderson, this rhetorical judgment is meaningful: to advance our values, we must situate our judgment in our research, which ensures that we maintain our professional standing in reform.

To be clear, this critical view is not shared by all Symposium participants. Bruce McComiskey (2012) admits that he was prepared to hate the Common Core State Standards (CCSS) as something that would "tie teachers' hands behind their backs, forcing them to teach writing out of rhetorical context and in formulaic (modal, five-paragraph) structures" (537). But when he finds no such tendency in the standards, he admits is "puzzled" by the *Framework*. If no one thing in the Common Core's stated values is disagreeable, he asks, why are we responding? In fact, McComiskey sees the *Framework* as so similar to the CCSS that he doubts school boards would sense a need to inquire critically into the CCSS (538). Given these similarities, McComiskey concludes, the CCSS is not to be feared—but corporately designed assessments are (539).

These scholars' stances dramatize the redirection/critique split. For McComiskey, there is no apparent difference between the stated values formed by corporate-political reform and those formed by composition professionals. If the values are the same, teachers, scholars, and administrators can serve these values without compromise. Even if these values are framed within the logic of competition (both among students and among educational policy providers), we can still serve the public goods of composition. Like the scholars of reframing cited above, McComiskey suggests that we can redirect the discourse of reform without compromising our professional judgment and democratic aims. But for Hansen as well as Summerfield and Anderson, such redirection ignores how the discourse of reform displaces composition professionals from the policy development process. By not acknowledging this displacement, these scholars suggest, we encourage the tendency in reform debate to grant equivalence between our professional judgments and those of corporate-political service providers. Redirection compromises our professionalism, our discourse, our values; thus, these scholars argue, we need to say what we want, in our terms.

This standoff reappeared in the May 2012 issue of *CCC*, where several scholars responded to *Academically Adrift* (Arum and Roksa 2011) and the goals of the Collegiate Learning Assessment. Richard Haswell (2012) and Jeanne Gunner (2012) offer what might be considered conventional denunciations in their essays. Haswell dismisses the CLA's methodology as inappropriate to the claims it makes; Gunner questions *Academically Adrift*'s conception of education as a commodity. Both appeal to professionalism to highlight the inadequacy of reform, arguing implicitly we need the right people to apply the right methods with the right purposes. However, the other two reviewers, Carolyn Calhoon-Dillahunt (2012) and Theresa Redd (2012), offer less openly critical perspectives. Calhoon-Dillahunt (2012, 496) affirms *Academically Adrift*'s concerns with limited student learning but points out that *Adrift* invokes a student body that doesn't match up with the student body of most institutions.

Despite these disjunctions, she still calls on composition to take a position much like reframing. "Rather than resist Arum and Roksa's findings," Calhoon-Dillahunt argues, "we should embrace *Academically Adrift* for its focus on what matters most: learning. The book demonstrates the need for a more complete and coherent body of research that gives a full, rich picture of student learning and provides a valuable starting point for national dialogue on improving student learning on college campuses" (498–99). Although respondents to *Adrift* do not address each other, their position side-by-side dramatizes the rhetorical distance between redirection and critique. How might we read Calhoon-Dillahunt or Redd's qualified embraces through the lenses of Haswell's methodological critique or Gunner's suspicion of reform's commonplaces? Are scholars *not* being adequately critical when they take reform's invocations as starting points for participation in reform debate? Are scholars being insufficiently "pragmatic" when they pose problems to (or wholly discount) reform's methods of assessment? What form of professional rhetorical judgment, critique or reframing, best accounts for the exigency of contemporary reform? And how can we talk to each other about these judgments without falling into stalemate?

These are questions that proponents of reframing aim to address through the invocation of prophetic pragmatism. But rather than rewriting the polarities of the redirection/critique debate, reframing's pragmatism tends to reify them. The disciplinary conversations about the *Framework* and the CLA/*Adrift* demonstrate the consequences of such a pragmatism: we tend to talk past each other about what Bruce Horner (2015) calls the material social of composition, never fully engaging with the grounds of our colleagues' judgments about going public. Still, reframing opens a key question about our rhetoric of professionalism: what commitments do we share that might guide and coordinate our public responses to reform? And how might we develop a rhetoric of professionalism better suited to the constraints of the contemporary scene? What can extend this conversation, I believe, is an inquiry into pragmatism as a standard of rhetorical judgment. Reframing invokes two central practices in the philosophical pragmatic tradition: melioration, or the improvement of public problems, and prophetic critique. In the following section, I read the pragmatism enacted against the pragmatism invoked, seeking to understand how reframing selects, reflects, and deflects the vision of West and others. Through this analysis, I identify opportunities for reopening composition's disciplinary inquiry into going public.

ON PRAGMATIC MELIORISM

In the pragmatic tradition, the term for improvement is meliorism (Dewey 1927, 208; Jackson and Stroud 2014; Stob 2005; Stroud 2006; Stroud 2010). For contemporary rhetorical scholars of pragmatism like Scott Stroud (2006), meliorism represents the work of improving a situation despite limitations (287), particularly finding ways to improve the experience of those in difficult situations (Stroud 2010, 48). Likewise, Paul Stob defines meliorism as the faith that circumstances can be improved through human involvement (240). This effort at improvement has a specific focus: although the pragmatic tradition seeks to enact broad changes that improve public inquiry, deliberation, and cooperation, melioration tends to be linguistic. As Stob puts it, pragmatic criticism issues a "call to alleviate the public's problems through a reconstruction in language" (240), and the task of critics is "crafting linguistic solutions to specific problems [so that] life can get better." To solve public problems, the task of critics "is to reconstruct a specific thread in the discursive fabric that unites person to person in the public sphere" (241).

West (1989) forwards a specific method of improving public discourse. Prophetic pragmatism is a form of critical melioration, a "form of cultural criticism that attempts to transform linguistic, social, cultural, and political traditions for the purposes of increasing the scope of individual development and democratic operations" (230). In this view, improvement depends on critical provocations to "hold elites to account" (213), forward the experiences of ordinary people (214), and denounce the "evils of the day" (233), even when this denunciation authorizes ordinary people to oppose professionals and experts (182, 207). Indeed, for West, pragmatism's specific force comes from its antiprofessional quality: critics' role is to invite public inquiry into and critique of expert judgments made on public behalf. However, West is careful *not* to say that critics should simply denounce problematic discourse in public life. To be effective, West argues, critics must be *artful:* they must "think genealogically about specific practices in light of the best available social theories, cultural critiques, and historiographic insights and to act politically to achieve certain moral consequences in light of effective strategies and tactics" (209). To pursue artfulness, critics must re-evaluate their conventional rhetorics of critique against their likely consequences in particular contexts. Based on this contextual judgment, critics can seek ways to invite their specific audiences to reflect on the limits of exclusionary perspectives to reflect their experience.

If critique drives West's pragmatic melioration, why does reframing seek to manage critique in the name of pragmatism? Reframing arrives at this stance, I believe, by minimizing attention to West's qualifier of artfulness. If critique cannot be artful, melioration requires message discipline. But this conclusion also has its own likely consequences: it narrows teachers' and scholars' professional roles in responding to reform, for if we are incapable of artfulness and in need of message management, going public is limited to the redirection of reform discourse. As the previous section of this essay demonstrates, however, composition's diversity of perspectives on reform frustrates reframing's managerial aspirations. Another consequence may be more important still: redirecting reform can also narrow roles for our public audiences in responding to reform. While reframing attempts to re-establish teachers' and scholars' professional standing in era of reform, it forecloses on the potential of professional critique to sponsor public inquiry into and critique of reform's rhetorical style. This foreclosure recalls Bousquet's (2003) argument that a managerial pragmatism doesn't consider what it's like for teachers and scholars to be managed (28). I would extend this argument to the publics of composition: reframing doesn't consider what it's like to be the public to our professionalism if that professionalism is built on the redirection of reform's realist style.

If the goals of pragmatic meliorism are broader than composition's concern with defending professionalism amid reform, how might reframing be expanded to account for the public aims of the pragmatic tradition? For West, the central characteristic of pragmatic critique is its "antiprofessionalism," its invitation of public inquiry that can authorize or challenge expert policy decisions. As West (1989) puts it, "what was the prerogative of philosophers, i.e., rational deliberation, is now that of the people—and the populace deliberating is creative democracy in the making. Needless to say, this view is not a license for eliminating or opposing all professional elites, but it does hold them to account" (213). This stance would goad professionals to go public not only by redirecting or denouncing dominant perspectives but also by creating opportunities for public audiences to assess and critique these perspectives. This rhetorical judgment envisions going public as a process of public formation: the point of professionals responding to reform, in this light, is to sponsor critical public inquiry that can contend with the power of realist style. Accepting reframing's message discipline as the enactment of pragmatism, however, tends to direct our attention away from the antiprofessional public participation sought by the pragmatic tradition. Reframing's disciplining of critique aims to avoid one problem—professionals' critiques falling on reformers' deaf ears—but it contributes to another by reducing opportunities for our public audiences to experience the limitations of reform's conventionalized perspectives.

If reframing tends toward managing composition and its publics through message discipline, how might reframing be expanded to make room for artful critique? A starting point is the definition of critique itself. Reframing associates critique with unidirectional public intellectualism (Adler-Kassner 2008, 82), pointing out what is wrong without saying what's right

(Adler-Kassner and O'Neill 2010, 167), or saying that "writing can't be measured" (165). Yet in the melioristic and prophetic vein explored above, critique extends beyond the denunciation imagined in reframing. As Stroud and Stob argue, the point of such critique is to sponsor public inquiry that can demand terms more adequate to broader participation. Among composition scholars as well, critique is not *only* saying that "writing cannot be measured"; it is saying that writing is better measured by means other than the ones demanded by reform. If the practice of critique in the pragmatic tradition and in composition is not reducible to reframing's portrait of critique, how might critique advance the work of melioration and prophetic transformation?

In the pragmatic tradition, such a critique tends to scale down in order to scale up. Scaling down refers to critics' role in sponsoring local public inquiry. In *The Public*, Dewey (1927) calls on experts "break through the crust of conventionalized and routine consciousness" (184). To achieve such a goal, expert critique needs to do more than perform a rejection of a dominant perspective. Instead, Stroud argues, critics' task is to attend to their local audiences' experiences in concrete situations (Stroud 2011, 42). Based on this attention, critics can invite their audiences to reflect on the ways in which a conventional perspective does or does not reflect their experience (42). When audiences take on this orientation, they can experience their current situation as "problematic" (37). As Dewey (1935) argues in *Art as Experience*, "the value of [such an] experience is not only in the ideals it reveals, but in its power to disclose many ideals, a power more germinal and more significant than any revealed ideal, since it includes them in its stride, shatters and remakes them" (322). Local inquiry can point toward the need for change.

Here pragmatic critique, contrary to Adler-Kassner and O'Neill's (2010) claim that "pointing out what is wrong does not provide anyone a handhold for acting upon what is right" (167), attempts both a disintegrative and a re-integrative role. By inviting audiences to experience potential disjunctions between commonsense perspectives and their experiences, artful critique also stokes audiences' desire to *revise* their perspectives—to begin a process Walter Muyumba (2014) describes as "rearticulating, problematizing, and reconstructing the plural publics and cultures in which we find ourselves" (167). This reconstruction is local and individual, but such inquiry also has larger potential. If critics help publics "[tell] the tales of their own 'aesthetic' experience," Muyumba argues, these critics can help "generate the communication necessary for creating associations and knowledge regarding shared cultural or community experiences" (167). That is, the circulation of stories of local inquiry can serve the function of critique: they can invite other audiences to reflect on their own experiences as a way of problematizing reform's standardizing perspective. Dewey (1927) elaborates on this function in *The Public,* calling on critics to sponsor local public inquiry into shared concerns and then to circulate accounts of this inquiry more broadly (153). By sponsoring continuous inquiry into diverse contexts, Dewey argues, critics can help break up the calcifications of public discussion (184) and improve public discourse. In this view, local critique and experiences of inquiry can scale up to foster a broader public discussion of shared concerns.

Certainly, reframing attempts such a scaling down and scaling up. Amid the stalemates of national reform debate, proponents of reframing call on teachers, scholars, and administrators to respond sensitively to policy discussions. Artful critique, from reframing's view, does not decry potentially deprofessionalizing reforms but invites policy agents, such as testing companies, political think tanks, and administrators tasked with implementing reforms, into experiences that can disclose alternate perspectives and suggest the need for a revised approach to policy. Those who attended the 2015 CCCC in Orlando may recall such an invitation at the Dialogue on Success in Postsecondary Writing. Moderated by Les Perelman, this dialogue featured David Coleman, president and CEO of the College Board; John Williamson, executive director of Advanced Placement Curriculum Development at The College Board; Elyse Eidman-Aadahl, co-director of the National Writing Project; 2016 CCCC chair Adler-Kassner; and past CCCC chair Kathleen Blake Yancey. This invitation recognized the need for a starting place among seemingly irreconcilable perspectives. As Adler-Kassner and O'Neill (2010) put it, "while we might ultimately like to say we should take a more radical stance, defining precisely what *we* want and advocating for that at all costs, we know such a positioning would fall on deaf ears and ultimately cause more harm than good" (177).

Yet the deaf ears of those who control reform efforts are not the only audiences in public discussions of reform. Proponents of reframing implicitly conclude that professional critique of reform is not worth the trouble because the prospects for fostering public inquiry are slim. Thus, composition teachers, scholars, and administrators are better off redirecting reform in the hope of gaining a seat at the table than by inviting public inquiry into and critique of reform. This conclusion rightly recognizes that participants in reform debate speak from what Gerard Hauser (2014) calls "dialectically secured positions of progressive or neoliberal ideology that reduce political relations to a zero sum game" (235). Yet despite the stalemates that characterize the contemporary political economy, Hauser argues, critics' pragmatic potential is to sponsor "the rhetorical experience of diversity as a way of creating relationships through inquiry" (242). Scholars of reframing insist that they do this by redirecting the stated goals of the Common Core or the Collegiate Learning Assessment. And they do. An artful critique guided by West's critical melioration, however, would *also* seek to enlarge policy debate so that a broader range of public audiences can experience the limits of reform discourse to reflect their experiences with literacy. Publicly fostering such antiprofessional possibilities is the aim of an artful critique.[2]

TOWARD A PRAGMATIC PUBLIC CRITIQUE

I opened this chapter by dramatizing the clash between reframing and the Human Readers petition. Both are concerned with the capacity of going public to advance professionalism, and both forward tactics for the contemporary moment:

denunciation or redirection. But both tactics also tend to fall into conventionalized appeals: only professionalism can serve the public good; only redirection recognizes the way the world is. While these perspectives anticipate the very real constraints of contemporary debate, their rhetorical styles begin to form a circle. In its attempt to redirect the market discourse of reform, proponents of reframing forward a realist style of their own: like it or not, *this* is what we have to do in the world we all inhabit (see Adler-Kassner and O'Neill 2010, 88). And embraces of critique assume that reasserting professional practice as public responsiveness is sufficient to break the stalemates of contemporary reform debate.

Certainly, these assumptions may bear out, but they are not certainties. Reframing's redirection of realist style may well create space for composition's professional values amid reform, but such judgment may also accelerate the neoliberalization of writing expertise. We don't know. Despite avoiding the terms bureaucracy and management, scholars of reframing advance a similar argument, except that the pragmatism of reframing is framed as prophetic, not managerial. As I've argued here, however, the prophetic aims of reframing are limited by a rhetorical style designed to defend professional standing.

In taking up this move, reframing tends to shortcut its pragmatic provocation. The case for reframing recognizes the limits of our conventional rhetoric of professionalism in the contemporary reform scene. Asserting the mistakenness of corporate-political reform and the rightness of experts appears to do little to reopen stalemated debates. Sensing this standoff, proponents of reframing invite us to envision a public rhetoric of professionalism for composition. That is, reframing seeks to make the grounds of professional judgment accessible so that composition's pluralistic contextualism can be affirmed not only as the exercise of expertise but also as the democratic representation of our publics' experiences with writing. This is the work West, Dewey, and other pragmatists envision professionals undertaking in an effort to build publics' capacities for democratic participation. But by encouraging us to work publicly within the terms of reform, reframing discounts the power of realist style to narrow and constrain the participation of the publics served by reform. And by disciplining our public critique, reframing discourages us from one means of tapping into the public inquiry and participation that could authorize our professionalism as publicly representative.

This is not to say that critique necessarily engages public participation, however. By denouncing machine scoring's methodology as a public problem and forwarding professional judgment as a solution, HR falls back on our familiar argument that professional judgment is the bulwark of democracy. Again, while this is our favored appeal, such an argument appears not to unsettle the dominance of realist style or reopen reform debate. Rather than endorsing critique over reframing, then, I am suggesting that HR's public critique deserves a look beyond reframing's message discipline because it may demonstrate a potential strategy for going public. In addition to denouncing assessment methodologies central to reform, many of the scholars cited in the HR petition perform their critical inquiry into an act of assessment, inviting their audiences to examine their own experiences with assessment through the same lens.

Les Perelman's (2014) *Boston Globe* article "Flunk the Robo-graders" demonstrates such a performance.[3] Perelman begins with an example of nonsensical prose: "*According to professor of theory of knowledge Leon Trotsky, privacy is the most fundamental report of humankind. Radiation on advocates to an orator transmits gamma rays of parsimony to implode*" (emphasis in the original). Perelman then says what readers are thinking: "any native speaker over age 5 knows that the preceding sentences are incoherent babble." But machines don't know this; in fact, as Perelman explains, they rated this prose highly. This concern is not merely an academic one, however. As Perelman points out, machine scoring is at the heart of the new assessments for the Common Core. So, the question of writing assessment is a public and national one. And the issue of machine scoring is the failure of its methodology to understand how writing works: "Robo-graders do not score by understanding meaning but almost solely by use of gross measures, especially length and the presence of pretentious language." When metrics are this poorly designed, they can be gamed. Who then should read student writing? Perelman proposes having expert teachers check at least 20 percent of the papers evaluated by machine readers, arguing that "education, like medicine, is too important a public resource to allow corporate secrecy."

Perelman performs his inquiry into machine scoring and concludes with a familiar peroration: we need professionals to serve the public good. But I suggest this inquiry can also be performed to sponsor critical public participation in local contexts. This participation is already happening among students and parents involved in the Opt Out movement. As *The New York Times* reported in May 2015 (Harris and Fessenden 2015), parent-teacher organizations, teachers' unions, and superintendents have sponsored such public attention to the new assessments that New York Governor Andrew Cuomo is reconsidering his embrace of testing. Granted, public decisions to opt out may center on methods of writing assessment or on broader consequences of standardized measures. But one impact of this engagement is clear. Our concern about *who* should define the goals and measures of literacy education is being taken up as an issue worthy of public as well as professional participation.

The relative success of Opt Out suggests the possibility of a parallel effort in composition. When we create opportunities for parents, teachers, and administrators to assess the assessments, our critiques of machine scoring may not only issue expert denunciations but also foster public participation in reform. Although movements to opt out do not counter the realist style of reform in national debate, they do foster local critiques that unsettle the inevitability of reform and may potentially authorize composition's professional perspectives. Such local public critique, fragmented and contingent as it is, appears to have a greater impact on reform debate than the professional statements we make in composition. As assessments such as those championed by Complete College America come more fully into view, we will need to begin thinking about going public not only as decrying or redirecting reform but also as sponsoring critical public participation in the questions of reform.

DEVELOPING A (PRE)RESPONSE TO THE CCA

One key question of contemporary reform is what students need to move through college more quickly. In *Time is the Enemy* (Complete College America 2011), CCA lays out proposals for accelerating completion. The first step, CCA argues, is to establish common measures of student readiness for entering their majors and their programs. With this data, better decisions can be made at the state level: governors can "allocate funds appropriately, measure the progress of postsecondary performance over time, encourage successful practices, and discourage waste in the postsecondary system." Although CCA does not name first-year writing (FYW) as a central concern, the "pre-major learning" emphasized in CCA happens in FYW. And while CCA avoids saying exactly *how* it plans to speed students along, the available public documents suggest that CCA's sights are set on a standardized FYW equivalency assessment. It takes little effort to imagine "innovative" course delivery modules that would allow students to demonstrate writing development equivalent to FYW *without taking FYW*.

Early in its development, CCA considered Accuplacer, the College Board's computer-based placement software for incoming first-year students, as a means of measuring students' readiness for their major coursework. That is, CCA saw Accuplacer as a potential equivalency exam for FYW. But starting in 2011, CCA began to critique Accuplacer for reasons familiar to us in composition: they argued that the test doesn't tell us about students' abilities, it can land students in non-credit-bearing courses that lengthen students' time to degree, and it forward criteria for "college-level writing" that do not align with actual college writing (Headden 2011). Even though CCA now positions itself in opposition to Accuplacer, CCA offers no evidence that they offer anything substantially different. In this situation, I believe our existing inquiries into Accuplacer and other machine scoring platforms can help us anticipate CCA's proposals. Rather than starting from scratch, in other words, inquiry into CCA might pick up where Patricia Freitag Ericsson and Richard Haswell's collection *Machine Scoring of Student Essays: Truth and Consequences* leaves off (Ericsson and Haswell 2006). The contributors to *Truth* offer a set of trenchant questions for assessing efforts at mass machine scoring. As Edmund Jones asks, does this assessment measure the actual skills of writing that matter in majors and programs (94)? Does this assessment treat writing, in Ericsson's memorable phrase, as "a bag of words" (Ericsson 2006, 32) to be scanned and counted? And does this assessment create "a black box" (Haswell 2006, 70) around the reading of student writing, as Richard Haswell finds most entrepreneurs of machine scoring doing?

If the answer to these questions is yes (as I suspect it will be), I am hopeful because our scholarship not only decries the poverty of machine-scored "meaning" but also invites local public engagement in questions of assessment. Tim McGee (2006), for example, describes how he performs his inquiry into the texts assessed by Pearson's Intelligent Essay Assessor for audiences at his institution (91). Like McGee (2006), Jones (2006) abstracts a scoring method from proprietary assessment software and then dramatizes the limits of this method to appreciate written meaning in his students' texts (109). For both McGee and Jones, the power of such local inquiry is that it dramatizes otherwise narrow debates about scoring methodologies. Such dramatizations are where I see assessment inquiry informing efforts at going public. Local audiences experiencing the limits of machine scoring to account for their meaning making can articulate a dual response to reform: yes, machine scoring fails to satisfy professional criteria, but it also falls short of public expectations for being read.

This possibility suggests a strategy for going public locally. We can invite our students to consider how they are being read through machine scoring criteria, and we can compare these inquiries to campus- and system-level administrators' rationales for using these tools. Placed side by side, these responses dramatize the distance between students' experiences with and administrators' arguments for machine scoring. In their contribution to *Truth*, Anne Herrington and Charlie Moran describe what we are likely to find if we take up this line of inquiry: students expressing concerns about experiences of being read (Herrington and Moran 2006, 118) while administrators appeal to cost and time savings (117), Following the lead of the Opt Out movement, I see an opportunity to circulate these local inquiries to sponsor broader public discussion of reforms like CCA. Students' inquiries into the experience of being read, especially when contrasted with administrators' rationalizations of machine scoring, can disclose the limits of "efficiency" and "cost-effectiveness" for governing the work of reading and responding to student writing.

Proposals for this sort of circulation need further discussion. What are likely consequences for professionals whose college-campus-, and system-level administrators are tasked with implementing major-readiness assessments? Whose concerns are being represented here—ours? Our students'? And what prevents the circulation of student inquiry from collapsing into the usual end-game of reform debate—the contextualism of professionalism trumped by the cost-effectiveness of standardization and mechanization? The question of consequences for contingent and untenured faculty is serious, but I believe that teachers, scholars, and administrators can contribute to the effort of going public without being outed by our antiprofessional circulation. The situations I described in chapter 2 suggest that students' interest in reform can arise from our teaching. Over time, we can anticipate these moments and seek to extend them. That is, we can consciously sponsor students' inquiry into reform judgments made on their behalf. That is the form of antiprofessional participation and contribution I envision for most of us—myself included. I see teaching professional writing as an occasion for performing my inquiry into reform arguments about students' needs as writers.

The question of whose interests are served by the circulation of student inquiry is equally serious. I anticipate little disagreement among us in composition over whether machine-scored

FYW equivalency exams are likely to prove adequate to assessing students' readiness to enter their majors. (I'd sooner anticipate us posing problems to the notion of "major readiness" assumed by CCA.) But we are rightfully squeamish of "astroturfing" student dissent. I explore this question more fully in chapter 5, but for now, I acknowledge that our role in sponsoring, stylizing, and circulating student inquiry is ambiguous. We forward what are legitimately public concerns with assessment. Under CCA, students' writing will in all likelihood be measured reductively, and reductive measures will in all likelihood limit access for our most vulnerable students. We have a ready response to this concern, of course, but its style is conventional: we need the contextualism of professional judgment to address the diversity of our publics' experiences with literacy and writing. Circulating student inquiry into standardization attempts to sidestep the usual standoff that arises from our idealist-style objections to proposals for FYW equivalency.

Some of us may have already attempted to go public in this fashion and already heard the following response on our campuses, in our state systems of higher education, or in discussions with state leaders: certainly, we agree that it'd be better to have more professionals reading student writing, but we simply can't afford the cost. This turn of argument illustrates that, while an alternate realist style may break the stalemate between idealist style and the appeals of reform, the antiprofessional circulation of student inquiry is not assured as a defense of our professionalism. So, while I highlight the potential of students' inquiry into the machine scoring of their writing to articulate dissent toward reform, such dissent might not sponsor the larger critical public discussion that could authorize our professional judgment as adequate to the complexity of writing. And such public discussion, if it happens, may or may not redound to our professional standing.

These contingent possibilities bring us back to the grounds of reframing's pragmatic inquiry. Without reference to what I've called idealist style, proponents of reframing recognize the limits of denunciation as a part of our conventional rhetoric. That is, we denounce because we assert that we are required to serve the public good. But in their inquiry and innovation, proponents of reframing decide not to wager now on the possibilities of public participation. Perhaps proponents of reframing wisely reserve such possibilities for another occasion *after* attempting redirection. Amid the uncertainties of contemporary reform, such wisdom may well bear out. But perhaps what we face now—the antiprofessionalism of movements like Opt Out—*is* an opportunity to develop a new public conversation. Perhaps our students' inquiry *can* foster the kind of public discussion that has slowed the rush toward Common Core implementation. If this is the case, we will need to consider the potential for artfulness in our critique. Perhaps it can do more than denounce.

If our public critique can be artful, we don't need to manage critique. What we do need, I believe, is to find ways of inviting each other to contend with the possibility of artfulness. This is the stylistic tough-tender pivot I introduced at the outset of this book. In *The Public*, Dewey (1927) suggests one such bid for reopening our conversation. He worries, much like composition teachers, scholars, and professional associations today, that the gulf between experts and publics is "being bridged not by the intellectuals but by investors and engineers hired by captains of industry" (205). Unless professionals learn to engage their publics more effectively, Dewey warns, informed public participation in public policy will likely be eclipsed by consumer choice. Yet Dewey argues that the task of professionals facing the threat of displacement by markets is not to reappropriate the conventionalized appeals of bureaucracy and markets but to refashion professionalism as responsiveness to public experience. As we seek to go public amid the present of market-driven reform, Dewey reminds us that our professional standing is contingent on its publicness. And, Dewey challenges us to envision a rhetoric of professionalism adequate to public participation and engagement.

Perhaps Dewey's worry reads like just more tough-mindedness about markets and tender-mindedness about public potential. In other words, it may sound like I've recovered a Dewey favorable to Bousquet and critical of Miller. But I read Dewey more like a bid to appreciate the limits of management and competition for our aims. The Deweyan view is long, to be sure, and we may never reach it. In that eventuality, reframing helpfully foreshortens the horizon to engage pragmatic inquiry in the present. But Dewey also points out what may be possible beyond the horizon of redirection. Artful critique is one method of enacting a public rhetoric of professionalism for the long game. As this chapter has explored, however, methods alone are not enough to reopen conversation in composition. What we need, I argue, is a style for inviting each other into inquiry regarding the uncertainty of our rhetorical judgment. What might make us want to consider an alternate understanding of the political economy of reform? In the following chapter, I explore an effort by scholars to formulate such a style, both within the discipline and in responses to reform. Its invitation is less that of discipline than of participation. The innovation of public engagement is that of broadening who speaks for professionals. In Dewey's vision, our spokespeople are not only ourselves but our publics who would authorize our "thereness"—our locality and our judgment in context. Speaking for ourselves so that others may also speak for us is the aim of the innovation explored in the next chapter.

BUT FIRST, THE ELEPHANT IN THE ROOM

This chapter's outlook reflects a moment (2014–16) when neoliberal reform appeared to be slowing. The energy of the Common Core was dissipating in the face of public and political resistance, and the ambitions of the Collegiate Learning Assessment appeared to have been stymied by the AAC&U's redirection of the Voluntary System of Accountability. Even Complete College America was being reappropriated as a warrant for *increasing* rather than *cutting* state funding to higher education.[4] Today, however, these reforms seem almost quaint. At least they gestured toward democratic rationales for the standardization of educational expertise and competition among service providers of this expertise. Now, if Education Secretary

Betsy DeVos's confirmation process was any indication, choice has superseded equity as the encompassing rationale for contemporary reform.

Yes, DeVos (2017) invokes equity when she argues that the denial of school choice to poor students constitutes "not just an issue of public policy but of national injustice." But DeVos's paean to choice never acknowledges the sources of judgment that might supply a marketplace of service providers focused on delivering educational justice. Nor does she discuss the quality of this judgment. Rather, DeVos suggests that we would do better to change the conversation from questions of expertise to questions of freedom. Once we stop focusing on "what the system thinks is best for kids," she argues, we can more fully focus on "what moms and dads want, expect and deserve." In this vision, educational expertise, at least at the K–12 level, does not appear to be marketized so much as dispersed through consumer and cultural choice.

Certainly, the DeVos confirmation process was disheartening, and it suggested that the scene for going public has changed. But I don't believe the present scene should be read as a reason to discount the potential of the antiprofessionalism described in this chapter and others. Indeed, our publics *do* appear to be seeking opportunities to authorize expert judgment for its capacity to deliver democratic goods. There is broad support for the courts' role in slowing administrative efforts like the travel ban (Burns 2017). Women's marches have gathered vocal public resistance to policy changes ranging from immigration to reproductive rights to racial justice to science.[5] And senators' offices across the country have been flooded with calls protesting the DeVos confirmation.[6] But of course, that confirmation and a suite of regressive policy changes have gone ahead anyway. These trends may be reversed, but in the meantime, they prompt us to consider yet another turn in our conversation on going public, a turn that might take us beyond the conclusions of this chapter. If the next rounds of critical public engagement fall on deaf ears, how might we proceed? What kinds of judgments about consequences should guide our rhetorical judgment and action? By articulating an alternate pragmatism in this book, I have suggested a way to reassess composition's denunciations and redirections of reform as wise judgments about consequences. But I also anticipate an alternate pragmatism goading us to reassess this chapter's call for public inquiry and resistance. Given what we can see now of the emerging reform landscape, what should we do?

Again, by asking this question in early 2017, I am not foreclosing on the potential of antiprofessional public engagement. That potential might arise from continued resistance to the policies of the Trump administration. But I am anticipating that we may also discover other resources for going public as we negotiate the changing landscape of reform. For example, I can see how we might find ourselves reconsidering our stance toward appeals to "choice." I don't mean that we'll want to try redirecting such appeals because we now have reason to believe that doing so may help us secure material and policy consequences. Rather, I mean that the prominence of "choice" may help form inquiry-driven counter publics. If the January 2017 women's march is representative, public expressions of resistance to "reform" appear to be gathering and amplifying a range of adjacent concerns. If it's not machine scoring or standardization that motivates critical public participation in reform, then, it may be professionals' persistent willingness to grapple with multiple forms of difference. Granted, public resistance to the dispersal of *our* expertise has not yet materialized, but that resistance may arise from a set of related concerns about professionals' judgment in context. In the present moment, "choice" *might* enable public resistance to what Dewey (1927, 205), calls "rule by an economic class." And this resistance *might* confront the next rounds of reform with public authorizations of professional judgment.

I recognize that this reading of consequences doubles back on the conclusions of the last chapter and this one. Like bureaucracy and reframing, this reading anticipates that we may discover new rationales for reappropriating and redirecting the appeals of reform. Today, however, "choice" appears even less encompassing than, say, "access" or "career- and college-readiness" may have seemed a few years ago, so "choice" talk feels even more jarring than reframing's efforts to enlarge the "porous narrative" of recent reforms. But, if an alternate pragmatism prompts us to attend to public experiences with rhetoric about literacy education, we may find "choice" creating a new exigency for our publics' inquiry into and critique of the educational judgment underlying reform.

At the same time, I recognize the constraints surrounding a democratic recuperation of "choice." Public groundings for our professional standing have vexed histories in composition. As the January 2016 special issue of *College English* demonstrates, the potentials of basic writing, community engagement, and language difference pedagogies have risen and fallen with the tides of political-economic change (see Cushman 2016; Gilyard 2016; Trimbur 2016). In light of our history, then, it should be clear that inviting public engagement guarantees no affirmation of professional judgment. But I do see a reason for hope in our current moment: public attention to the grounds of judgment *excluded* from the next generation of reform may clarify the public goods served by what Ellen Cushman (2016) calls composition's "emancipatory projects" (239). In response to this attention, we might go public by inviting further inquiry into (and a choice among) the judgments that claim to serve public goods. Following Keith Gilyard (2016), we might adopt the translingual wager on our publics' capacity to appreciate our judgment as a recognition of "the normal transactions of daily communicative practice of ordinary people" (212). From this view, an alternate pragmatism of going public would articulate our professionalism as a responsiveness to public experience—with the recognition that this experience may affirm as well as challenge our professional standing.

This rhetoric of professionalism would approach what Kenneth Burke (1984a, 107) calls "comic" critique: it would recognize the limits of conventional professional denunciations of reform, of efforts to reframe reform, and even of efforts to sponsor public inquiry into reform. An emancipatory recovery of "choice" would be comic, but I believe it could also be embold-ening for the work of going public. When our professionalism looks more and more like the fostering of public resistance to market dispersals of expertise—not just of our own but that of other professionals as well—we may find ourselves joining with others around terms we wouldn't otherwise seek out. Surely, we in composition will contest each other's judgment over this decision. And we may well reverse our course(s) with another administration: maybe reform will swing back from the "choice" of DeVos to the standardization-for-competition-for-justice of the Obama era, and if so, we'll have a draft of a strategy. But even then, we'd face a new set of uncertainties. In this light, the larger point of reassessing "choice" is not so much setting future terms for going public as it is reopening inquiry into the judgments about consequences we invoke to guide the work of going public. While an alternate pragmatism helps us chal-lenge these judgments, it does not *answer* the question of how to respond in a specific moment. Rather, it reminds us that assess-ments of the consequences of going public are subject to new judgments in new contexts, and we may find new opportunities in the experience of assessing the available options, however unattractive they may seem from our current vantage point(s).

NOTES

1. Adler-Kassner and O'Neill also identify genre (152), locality (170), research (101), and inquiry and analysis (171–72) as promising sites for reframing.

2. I am drawing on Chris Gallagher's (2005) call for an "engaged profes-sionalism" that works against the sociological tendency of expert com-munities to insulate themselves from the publics they serve.

3. See also Maja Wilson's (2006) "Apologies to Sandra Cisneros," which dra-matizes the failure of machine scoring to appreciate genre, context, and tone in literary prose. Likewise, Anne Herrington and Charles Moran demonstrate the failure of assessment software to reflect the sociocogni-tive dimensions of undergraduate writing in the disciplines (Herrington and Moran 2001).

4. Complete College America's appeal to Republican governors has been clear. A system of performance funding promises a rationale for state executives seeking to cut funding to state institutions. But at my institu-tion, the adoption of CCA has actually authorized more requests for

funding. For example, my institution's statement on CCA explains that "an 89 percent increase in bachelor's degrees between academic year 2009–10 and 2019–20 will require significant increases in resources. If the six-year graduation rate climbs from 50 percent to 60 percent, the undergraduate student population will have to climb from 12,828 in academic year 2009–10 to 20,300 by academic year 2019–20, to achieve the goal of 4,374 degrees awarded . . . Keeping the student/faculty ratio at twenty-two would require an additional 338 faculty positions at an approximate annual cost of $33.8 million. Additionally, the operating, student service, and classified support increases linearly with the number of students, so the 58 percent increase in number of students would require an additional annual amount of $11.8 million in these services" (Office of the Provost 2017).

5.   As Amanda Hess (2017) puts it in her February 7 *New York Times Magazine* essay, the signs present at the Women's March on Washington dramatized the role of the women's movement in catalyzing multiple concerns from "REFUGEES WELCOME," "KEEP YOUR LAWS OUT OF MY VAGINA," and "BLACK LIVES MATTER," to "SCIENCE IS REAL" and "FLINT NEEDS CLEAN WATER."

6.   As the Reno Gazette-Journal reported (Richardson 2017), some callers tried as many as forty times to reach the office of Dean Heller (R-NV) on February 2, 2017.

Chapter 4

BEING THERE, GOING PUBLIC, AND "*THE* PROBLEM OF THE PUBLIC"

Engaging neoliberal reformers through a dialectical approach such as stakeholder theory is self-defeating because neoliberals already have installed their own "ultimate" hierarchical order. The task, then, is to provide a compelling case for an alternative ultimate order, one that asserts the primacy of faculty and students in the assessment scene.

—Chris Gallagher, "Being There: (Re)Making the Assessment Scene" (2011, 462)

In this passage, Gallagher (2011) asserts an alternate standard of rhetorical wisdom for going public. As professionals in composition, we are accustomed to thinking of ourselves as stakeholders in contemporary reform (462). Following a "stakeholder theory of power," we seek out compromise, debate, and collaboration with others in the reform scene, all in the faith that these efforts can advance our professional values amid profound constraints. But since stakeholders in the contemporary neoliberal scene are not equal, Gallagher argues, we deprofessionalize ourselves by seeking to "collaborate" with reformers. Rather than seek out a compromised position when going public, then, we need to break with the hierarchy of neoliberal reform (463). To make this break, we must assert a new principle of educational improvement—not accountability, which reduces our judgment to the dictates of the globally competitive scene, but "being there." Since we are there at locations and relations of local power (466), we can reclaim "the expertise and leadership of those who spend their professional lives

DOI: 10.7330/9781607326540.c004

with students, not administrators higher on the institutional org chart or remote testing experts" (470). Remaking the scene in this way, Gallagher argues, promises to "[invert] the neoliberal order, positing a *positive* correlation between primacy and proximity to, and direct involvement in, the core work of education—teaching and learning" (464).

In a departure from bureaucracy and reframing, being there evinces a tough-mindedness about the possibilities afforded by reappropriating and redirecting reform's appeals to bureaucratic standardization and market competition. These innovations on going public, Gallagher suggests, reify the scene of the global and its attendant hierarchy of agents and agencies. Standardization within the global marketplace, in other words, still accelerates marketization, even if we're doing the standardization ourselves. From this perspective, going public as Graff and Birkenstein or as Adler-Kassner et al. propose risks reducing professionals to market share-seekers within the political economy of reform. The counterpart to this tough-mindedness is a tender-mindedness about the potential for our efforts at going public to sponsor broader resistance to neoliberal reform. Gallagher envisions educational unions and activist organizations as potential partners in reasserting the centrality of teachers and students in reform (469). If we dispense with the stakeholder theory of power, then, we can recognize our epistemic advantage in making judgment on the public's behalf. What we need next are ways of communicating our publicness so it can be recognized and affirmed.

Amid contemporary reform, this line of argument sounds like what I've called idealist style: the argument that our expert judgment in context ensures the democratic representation of our diverse publics. And in composition's disciplinary debate, being there sounds like a reversal of the tough and tender stylings forwarded by proponents of bureaucracy and reframing. A suspicion of reform's market realism, as outlined by Marc Bousquet, returns to undercut Richard Miller's (and others') hope for a more "pluralistic" rhetoric of professionalism. If we disagree with reform, then, we should say what we mean, in our own terms. Being there makes these rhetorical gestures, I argue, but it also extends them. By turning to activist networks outside our professional channels, being there acknowledges the sociological limits of expertise. We need to go public, but we need more people speaking on our behalf as well. Rhetorically, we need a new means of communicating locality that also allows a broader range of people to participate in the circulation of images of this locality. In this way, being there takes on the task I've described in this book—scaling down to scale up. Although Gallagher does not term his approach public engagement, his turn to activist networks envisions public participation as a means of unsettling the neoliberal order.

But this effort, as Gallagher admits, focuses mostly on the "inventional value of network logic" (469)—that is, what we can do conceptually and rhetorically within composition to go public. To scale up from being there, Gallagher suggests, we will likely need to work with the various "network structures" that can circulate accounts of our judgment. A key figure in this work, Gallagher suggests, are students (470). If students are central to being there, what role might students play in our going public? And how might we and students communicate what they do? These are the questions I explore in this chapter, particularly given my ongoing critique of idealist style's potential as a public rhetoric of professionalism amid the stalemates of contemporary reform debate. I share Gallagher's tough-mindedness toward the possibilities of reappropriating and redirecting the appeals of the neoliberal order. And I am similarly tender-minded about activism's potential to foster public authorizations of professional thereness. But I am skeptical about how we communicate what we do and what students do. While I agree that being there matters, I anticipate it, as a professional claim, falling into the familiar stalemate of reform debate between realist and idealist style. "Being there" means that *we* are there, and as I argue in this chapter, our claims of thereness are being displaced by reform's competing claims to be "there," or to exercise contextual judgment. Still, I believe, we can extend the pragmatic innovation of being there by elaborating its rhetorical performance. My question is how we might not only assert that being there matters but also dramatize it. This, I believe, is where student inquiry can come into play. A circulation-based perspective on going public takes scaling down as an opportunity for scaling up. Being there matters, certainly, but I see its value as contingent upon its likely consequences. The aim of being there is to sponsor other experiences of thereness, and for that to happen, we need our logic to be intelligible more broadly outside our field.

To support this effort, I situate being there among a set of adjacent inquiries. The public turn of community engagement highlights the participatory aims implicit in Gallagher's vision for going public. Mike Rose's focus on the concrete experiences of teaching and learning suggests a method for performing our "thereness" for our local publics. Dewey's vision of scaling down to scale up authorizes us to circulate accounts of our publics' local inquiry. And the pragmatic value of artfulness goads us to style accounts of local inquiry that do more than affirm professionalism as a public good. These inquiries, I argue, can help us extend being there to enact the participatory professionalism Dewey envisions. But such tactics can also unsettle professionalism by opening up our judgment to the inquiry of a broader range of people. The dilemma of going public, in this light, is the wager on antiprofessionalism to advance the values of professionalism. I appreciate being there as an engagement with this dilemma and seek to complement its rhetorical tactics for inviting the participation of our publics in reform.

DEFENDING PROFESSIONALISM BY DEMOCRATIZING IT

Gallagher's being there joins a long-standing project in composition. At least since *A Nation at Risk*, going public has sought to counter reform's totalizing invocations of market competition (Adler-Kassner 2008; Gallagher 2007; Gere 1991; Hull 2001; Trimbur 1991). As Mike Rose (1995, 245) argues, the national discourse of reform emphasizes standards, skills, and competitiveness while discounting alternate educational values, such as access and opportunity. Such a discourse prevents what Rose calls a "capacious critique" of public education, "one that encourages both dissent and invention, fury and hope" (4). To enable such a critique, Rose argues, "we need an expanded vocabulary, adequate to both the daily joy and daily sorrow of our public schools. And we are in desperate need of rich, detailed images of possibility." For Rose, we can begin reopening reform debate by displacing the dominant discourse—global competitiveness as the warrant for standardization and centralization—because this discourse prevents public inquiry into the specific contexts of teaching and learning to which professional judgment responds (98). Such an improvement is imagined to support not only democracy but our professionalism as well: public inquiry into specific and diverse contexts represents a potential source of support for our expert judgment against reform's demands for standardization and centralization.

However, this call to form local, inquiry-driven publics amid national reform debate confronts the tension I identified in the introduction of this book. How might we invite public participation, and how might we guide it without reducing it to professional self-promotion? These questions suggest a bridge between two discussions usually considered separately in composition. There is the explicit issue of this book: going public, or the theory and practice of advancing composition's professionalism amid neoliberal reform. But there is also community engagement—the theory and practice of forming local inquiry-driven counterpublics. These latter efforts, focused on what Eleanor Long (2008) calls "structural issues of poverty, illiteracy, and social fragmentation" (49), tend not to address professionals' standing to define the goals and measures of public education in literacy. Rather, public engagement and going public are kept separate based on a sense that professional standing should be a secondary concern in the community context. Ellen Cushman (1999) offers a representative view of this separation when she argues that while academics need to defend their own standing in an era of reform, "the fight for our own autonomy is a limited and self-serving form of political action addressed only to an elite 'public' of decision-makers" (329). Instead of focusing on elite publics to achieve professional goods, Cushman (2003, 171) insists, we should seek to combat the devaluation of local knowledge by increasing public access to representation in public conversations (174). In this view, *we* are not an underserved public; public engagement is for public goods, not professional goods.

These boundaries are qualified slightly in Linda Flower's (2008) *Community Literacy*. While Flower does not suggest we use public engagement to defend professionalism, she does not oppose professional and public goods. Professionals can create opportunities for ordinary people—not policymakers or think tanks—to inquire into problems they identify. Specifically, Flower argues, we can create opportunities for people to "unpack the experiential reality behind abstract claims" about public issues (36). We can then help people use this local knowledge to "transform understanding in a public deliberation." The professional good of community literacy—"a rhetorical competency that goes beyond empathetic disposition, assertive advocacy, or rational argument"—furthers the public good of improving deliberation. In moving "from researcher to public rhetorician," Flower argues, "we are able to use institutional authority to give a public presence to the people and perspectives without authority" (224). Thus, public purposes inform where and how professionals go public.

This vision of democratic engagement does not address the role of public engagement in supporting composition teachers', scholars', and administrators' professional standing amid reform. Indeed, the call to community literacy demonstrates what Cornel West (1989) calls the antiprofessionalism of the pragmatic tradition (182, 207), the tendency of contextual inquiry and public participation to exceed conventional professional hierarchies and boundaries. Accordingly, the call to community literacy urges professionals to broaden the focus of composition from the disciplinary to the literacies and experiences of "ordinary people" in specific social contexts. Yet Steve Parks and Eli Goldblatt, in "Writing Beyond the Curriculum," imagine the antiprofessionalism of public collaboration as a potential rhetoric of professionalism (Parks and Goldblatt 2000). Reconceiving writing to combine disciplinary and public literacy experience, they argue, could create more institutional commitment to the literacies of their local publics (585–86). Echoing Rose's call for a "capacious critique," Parks and Goldblatt imagine that such a "network of people concerned with literacy in a region could develop a supportive and constructive critique of public education that would make solutions possible across traditional educational and community boundaries" (588). The image of teachers, scholars, and administrators improving learning at all levels becomes a way for us to explain—to local and more distant audiences—why our research and pedagogy matter to the public more broadly. If composition thinks "strategically" about its partnerships, as Goldblatt (2005, 282) suggests elsewhere, one possible professional benefit of local reciprocity is that it can redefine professionalism as responsiveness to and engagement with local community. Such an approach resembles Kathy Fleischer's (2000) argument, in *Teachers Organizing for Change*, that when teachers are ignored, public audiences can speak on their behalf (3). Goldblatt (2007, 2) calls this kind of strategic thinking composition's "foreign policy." With outsiders "much more likely to ask questions about outcomes and make demands on our programs," and with such interrogations "often framed in the jargon of professional outcomes and managerial efficiency," Goldblatt calls on us in composition to articulate alternate values—the local, relationships, collaboration, complexity—and to ground them in concrete examples.

Although Goldblatt does not elaborate on the K–16 reforms he references (12), he envisions a response to a situation like the present, in which composition's local, experiential, and collaborative efforts are subsumed by the dominant discourse of reform. Thus, while community literacy and community collaborations reflect the antiprofessionalism of public participation, such efforts also build what Long (2008) calls "local publics" (16) whose trust in professional judgment can be leveraged to support our professional standing against the deprofessionalization of reform's standardization and centralization. Here composition's search for a public rhetoric of professionalism—one that both invites participatory inquiry *and* circulates this inquiry beyond the local—takes on what Dewey (1927) calls "*the* problem of the public": improving "the methods and conditions of debate, discussion, and persuasion" (208; emphasis in the original). Like the other professionals Dewey mentions, we in composition seek to sponsor local public inquiry and communicate our publics' findings (153). By sponsoring continuous inquiry into diverse contexts, we attempt to break up the calcifications of public discussion (184). The search for local knowledge—and the effort to inform broader conversations—is understood as a means of creating collaborative relationships among professionals and their publics (205). Going public via public engagement refigures professionalism as the sponsorship of antiprofessional public inquiry and critique.

As Dewey acknowledges, however, such a refiguring is complex. Experts *can* inform public participation to improve deliberation, and improved deliberation *can* bridge gaps between professional expertise and democratic participation. Broader public participation in policy concerns, however, can also *undermine* expert judgment. As Dewey notes, the gulf between expert knowledge and public participation in policy debates is now "being bridged not by the intellectuals but by investors and engineers hired by captains of industry" (205). Public participation in policy debates, then, may *affirm* the policies forwarded by corporate interests. Despite this risk, Dewey wagers on public-professional collaboration to satisfy the public need for locality. It is this locality that brings diverse experiences to bear on ostensibly representative judgments about public goods. And, for Dewey, it is the experience of this locality that has the potential to scale up and sponsor similar inquiries in different contexts.

This is the potential that I have invoked throughout this book—that antiprofessional public participation can potentially authorize our judgment as writing professionals. But as in Dewey's context, such an innovation on going public presents both opportunity and risk. For professionals, the local is often what we foreground to dramatize the failure of contemporary reforms to account for the diverse literacy experiences of our students and our publics. In the previous chapter, for example, I forwarded the locality of machine scoring as a means of inviting broader public participation in contemporary reform debate. A turn to the local, however, can also frustrate our defenses of professionalism: local inquiry into literate acts may affirm reform proposals for standardization and marketization rather than support our appeals to pluralism. Still, the broader wager of scaling down is that the diversity of public experiences with literacy will point toward the need for pluralism as a more adequate form of public representation, *even if* this pluralism doesn't redound to our conventional professional standing.

In an essay marking the NCTE's 2010 centennial, John Mayher, former NCTE president and a leader in the NCTE's standards efforts during the early 1990s, illustrates this pragmatic rhetorical judgment. In his response to the then-developing Common Core Standards Initiative, Mayher (2010) begins by enacting what I have called idealist style, insisting that "the only way fully to resist the reductive effect of [standardized] tests on English language arts teaching and learning . . . is to return to classroom teachers the central role in assessment they once had" (407). In terms of Dewey's concerns, Mayher makes his case clear. To serve the public good, literacy professionals and not think tanks or testing companies must constitute the community of inquiry informing policy. Professionalism *is* public representation.

Yet Mayher qualifies this stance by reading the process of defining "common" standards as an opportunity to sponsor public inquiry into reform. If we professionals are to represent our publics adequately, we will need to invite a broad range of perspectives on the following questions:

> what should be common? What could be individualized? Who has a voice in the decision making? How do we continue to build the community necessary to sustain a free democracy while at the same time maximizing the chance of each child to develop his or her own interests and talents to the fullest? Such a national

> revisioning would threaten the educational status quo and would
> undoubtedly be resisted by many, including, potentially, subject
> matter teachers and their organizations, even NCTE . . . What if a
> new vision of education suggests we don't need English teachers,
> or even literacy teachers, old or new? (411–12)

This inquiry, Mayher acknowledges, might affirm or challenge professional judgment. But like Dewey, Mayher commits to going public as a means of improving upon "*the* problem of the public." Going public is imagined as a way of reversing the "eclipse of the public," and this reversal, in turn, is valorized as a potential means of combatting the neoliberalization of literacy educators' expertise.

As Mayher's argument suggests, such a wager goads us in composition to attempt an alternate response to the political economy of reform. Like bureaucracy and reframing, a rhetoric of public engagement recognizes how the realist style of reform threatens to displace writing professionals and exclude public participation in debate. But unlike these other innovations on idealist style, a rhetoric of public engagement understands pragmatic judgment to encompass dissenting as well as managerial responses to reform's realist style. That is, going public via public engagement understands public participation as a means of unsettling the competitive world invoked by reforms like Common Core. Implicitly, a rhetoric of public engagement imagines a community of inquiry that extends beyond professionals and policy reformers to broader public audiences. Such a participatory professionalism seeks to sponsor local inquiry as part of a wager that public participation can authorize our critiques of totalizing perspectives on teaching, learning, and assessment. As a response to reform, public engagement seeks to transform the experience of public inquiry into a rhetoric of inquiry.

BEING THERE AMID CONTEMPORARY REFORM

This is the essential effort of being there—to communicate locality in a way that can sponsor new inquiries elsewhere, inquiries that can begin to reopen stalemated reform debate to a broader range of perspectives. Working from aims similar to Gallagher's, Linda Adler-Kassner (2008) forwards a tactic for circulating accounts of our locality. She urges us to "tell different stories about writing and writers"—stories showing that teachers can respond to and support student success using their contextual judgment. Likewise, the NCTE (Gardner 2010) calls on teachers to tell their stories to "take abstract notions and turn them into something concrete and compelling." In these cases, we tell stories of our judgment with the aim of unsettling the dominant narrative of reform and forwarding an alternate narrative. Even though Adler-Kassner and the NCTE do not associate realist style with reform and idealist style with professionalism as I do, their proposals recognize the need for an alternate rhetoric of professionalism. The central drama of these stories, the grounds that suggest more inquiry is needed, is the contrast of the conventional appeal of reform—standards for competitiveness—with the complex and varied realities of local experience. We scale down to scale up. But telling stories, like being there, represent familiar rhetorical strategies for teachers, scholars, and administrators in composition. How might accounts of thereness sponsor an experience of inquiry despite stalemated debates? And how might stories of our contextual experiences sponsor new inquiry in other contexts? Two examples may help answer these questions. The first example illustrates the challenges of circulating our thereness within the contexts common to contemporary reform.

In 2013, I attended a campus-wide meeting to discuss how the Smarter Balanced's Assessment Consortium (SBAC) would measure student performance on the Common Core Standards and how data from such assessments could help streamline the placement of students in our writing courses. Writing faculty and administrators were at the meeting, and we asked questions informed by the then-recent Human Readers petition against machine scoring (which SBAC uses). We asked representatives from SBAC and the chancellor's office of the Nevada System of Higher Education how they accounted for the limitations of machine scoring. What does this assessment of student writing tell us that we don't already know from classroom- and program-based assessments? In his response, however, Stanley Rabinowitz of WestEd dismissed our concerns on the grounds that the SBAC measured the key skills in a democracy. "You all want students prepared for democracy, don't you?" Rabinowitz asked. As we realized that SBAC interpreted democracy as access to skills through standardization, the limits of our appeal began to come into view. We had asserted the need to be there; in Burke's terms, we attempted to re-open discussion on the basis of agency: standardized testing and machine scoring of writing in particular represented not only a displacement of our judgment but also a public problem of bad judgment. To achieve the purpose of adequate understanding, then, we needed to change the agency. And of course, changing the agency meant changing the agents. We would need experts to get expertise.

After hearing our questions, Rabinowitz, more than a little peeved, pointed to the writing assessment on the overhead projector and asked, "well, don't you think these are good skills to develop?" The audience, K–16 across disciplines, nodded, apparently unconcerned that Rabinowitz had ignored our questions about standardization. Our effort to reopen debate on the grounds of the agency met with Rabinowitz's redirection from the agency to the purpose. To want democracy meant accepting standardization, and accepting standardization meant accepting agents other than professional teachers, scholars, and administrators in composition. Being there became a luxury the state and nation could ill afford in the push to increase democratic access to skills.

In reform discussions like this one from 2013, being there foregrounds the local, the contextual, and the experiential grounds of judgment. But *asserting* the need to be there did not invite the kind of openness to experience that being there seeks. Granted, this was a situation ill-suited to inquiry. Yet to foster experiences in our reform contexts, I believe being there needs a rhetorical means of sponsoring inquiry. In my and my colleagues' efforts to re-open discussion, we were looking for such a means. We avoided invoking the transcendent purposes of teaching and learning writing. Instead, we stuck to the agency as if we dispassionately insisted on Human Readers over machine scoring just because their judgment could more adequately reflect the complexity of the context. We asserted the need to be there not merely as the appropriate agency or policy, but a comprehensive reflection of act, agency, agent, scene, and purpose.

Amid the stalemates of debate, however, the conversation turned: being there was reduced to an agency, another means of judgment that could be interchanged with others. And since this agency stipulated agents—we who were there—being there encountered resistance as self-promotion on the part of professionals. Although we intended being there as an encompassing drama, it collapsed first into a bureaucratic plea for better methods, which then collapsed further into an idealist appeal for the right people. In short, while our invocation of thereness pointed toward a potentially public rhetoric of professionalism, it could only partly enact it. To develop such a rhetoric, we would need to articulate more specific rhetorical practices for sponsoring critical inquiry.

A similar experience with storytelling suggests that stories alone do not reopen inquiry amid stalemates. The NCTE's call to tell stories suggests that an account of the ways federal and state policies affect teaching, learning, and assessment can at least inform legislative decision-making and perhaps even steer it. Yet the potential for stories to sponsor inquiry depends on how teachers, scholars, and administrators negotiate the stalemates of debate. I found these stalemates deeper than the calls for storytelling would suggest they are. For example, in 2011, my institution began to adopt the "completion agenda," represented by Complete College America (CCA). CCA argues that low college completion rates hurt states' economic growth and should be addressed by implementing performance based funding based on standardized outcomes assessment in first-year writing, eliminating basic writing, delivering first-year courses online, and decreasing time to degree. The Nevada System of Higher Education (NSHE) endorsed CCA's goals and called for "partnership with K–12" to end remediation. This partnership would be implemented in a specific way: in Spring 2013, a pilot program began to remove UNR courses designated "remedial," and some sections of English 098, a basic writing course, would be taught in local district high schools by high school teachers.

For writing faculty at UNR, this practice raised questions: would high school teachers' understandings of student writing reflect the intent of the course ("basic" rather than "remedial")? What kind of preparation and support might teachers have when working with basic writers? And how might teachers adapt the 098 course (designed by faculty at UNR) to the high school context? These questions arose from basic writing scholarship. The removal of basic writing recalled the institutional responses of downsizing and restratification Mary Soliday (2002) identifies in *The Politics of Remediation.* When NSHE administrators suggested that underprepared students represented cost but not opportunity for the university, we heard echoes of the tendency Tom Fox (1999) terms choosing standards over access. And although no literacy educators have responded to CCA directly, our existing defenses of basic writing (e.g., Adler-Kassner and Harrington 2002; Horner and Lu 1999) highlight NSHE/CCA's lack of interest in student perspectives on writing, learning, and social context.

Since CCA was adopted by Nevada's governor, I attempted to tell the governor's office a story about how the adoption of the CCA was affecting instruction at UNR. I described how current students of mine, writing majors in capstone-level courses, started as basic writers in 098 (see chapter 2). Despite CCA's claims to be equipping students with skills for democratic access to opportunity, I made it clear that disinvesting in postsecondary basic writing was *not* supporting student access. As a story, I thought my drama had potential to sponsor inquiry: it began with the scene, my advanced writing course. In that scene, I specified, were several agents who had become majors and would graduate well-prepared to work in diverse fields. These students were so prepared because they had had access to the right means—English 098—at UNR. Thus, for the purpose of preparation for the workforce, Nevada needs the right means. These means, coincidentally, reflect the judgment of specific agents: professionals like me. The familiar drama emerged: to get expertise, you must have experts.

In retrospect, however, I can see that my focus on agency or means—which I assumed would demonstrate a dispassionate attention to outcomes—did not transform the other terms in debate. That is, while I emphasized the agency by telling a different story about writing and writers, I did not show how the alternate approach—pre-teaching remediation to pre-college students—would undermine the shared purpose of higher education access. In an effort not to critique the completion agenda on the basis of purpose (saying it undermined the democratic access it claimed to support) or the basis of agents (saying it ignored the expertise of educators who work with these students), I tried to play it bureaucratic. But in this case, my rhetoric of bureaucracy collapsed back into idealist style, because my case to the governor's office was that to address the scene effectively (many students arriving with varying levels of preparation), we need the right agency (basic, not remedial pedagogy), and to implement the right agency, we need the right agents: professionals.

What effect my input had is unclear; I received a perfunctory note of acknowledgment for my contact. In 2013, the decisions of state governors to sign on to Complete College America had already been politically secured and were not subject to new inquiry. Given the completion agenda's status as a proxy struggle over the relationship among markets and the state, I had no high hopes for storytelling as a means of going public. But given the stalemates of debate and the limits of conventional professional style as a response to reform, what can we say when going public? One way forward, I believe, is to reconsider storytelling as a form. Stories of our thereness demand that broader policy judgments made on behalf of the public reflect the local. But before we circulate such stories, we need to ask how their form might sponsor future inquiries in context. Dewey's approach to scaling up privileges accounts of inquiry that break up conventionalized communication—the stalemates I have emphasized in reform debate. Stories, at least from Dewey's perspective, need to dramatize experiences of local inquiry that can sponsor future experiences of inquiry in other contexts. We can tell stories that enact our conventional appeal, but this appeal risks reifying the stalemate of reform debate. Like being there, storytelling promises to reopen stalemated debates, but what storytelling offers debate is less a means of reopening than a form for circulating accounts of this reopening. Our practices of rhetorical invention, performance, and circulation require additional insight into what makes debate closed and how, particularly, stories of thereness can/could reopen the discussion.

DRAMATIZING THERENESS

When we attempt to improve the discourse of reform through local inquiry, we attend to the central theme of Dewey's (1927) *The Public*—professionals performing their inquiries and inviting their publics to reassess the publicness of policy judgments made on their behalf (142–48). Without explicit reference to Deweyan public formation, Mike Rose (1995, 2) suggests a means of transforming the local experience of inquiry into a national rhetoric of inquiry. Rose targets reform's "rhetoric of decline" and in particular, its "ready store of commonplaces" about failure. These commonplaces "[blind] us to complexity" and "attenuate [our] vision of the possible" to increased standardization and marketization. For Rose, performing our inquiry into specific contexts—into experiences with teaching and learning—can restore the depth and breadth to the national conversation on reform. Even though we may currently "lack a public critical language adequate to the task" (4), Rose suggests that we can build one through inquiry. The goal of going public as professionals, Rose argues, is to develop such a language. When we can return public discussion to the concrete experiences of teaching and learning (98), we can restore to public discussion a sense of our shared public experiences and goals (412) and education's "intellectual, social, civic, ethical, aesthetic" qualities (Rose 2009, 4).

Rose's efforts to represent and circulate accounts of contextual inquiry that unsettle "conventionalized" communication (Dewey 1927, 168) parallel what I've called an alternate realist style. Local inquiry into acts can disclose the complexity and diversity of scenes, agents, agencies, and purposes in literacy education. This diversity can unsettle reform's realist style of "competitive world, common standards." In a search for more adequate terms and perspectives for the experiences of teaching and learning, Rose suggests, public audiences may demand a broader perspective on reform, one not impoverished by the givenness of "the way the world is." In order to sponsor such public inquiry and critique of reform discourse, teachers and scholars need to circulate accounts of their judgment. But if this strategy points toward a way of scaling down to scale up, what is the local that we want to scale up?

In chapter 1, I noted how the seeming inevitability of the CLA has been stopped short by the AAC&U's reappropriation of demands from the Voluntary System of Accountability (VSA). Instead of standardizing and centralizing outcomes assessment for colleges and universities, VSA's reform appears more likely to happen in the contexts of practice. Without reference to Gallagher's argument, the AAC&U has effectively insisted that being there matters and has re-framed accountability as a matter of responsibility, to use Adler-Kassner and Harrington's (2010) terms. So while I have qualified the arguments of Adler-Kassner et al. in chapter 3, I certainly note the power of these scholars' logic in returning externally imposed reforms to the professional sphere of composition teachers, scholars, administrators. Redirection *can* advance our democratic capacity as professionals to represent our diverse publics.

Still, as I argued in chapter 1, it is hard *not* to anticipate the return of neoliberal standardization through reform schemes like performance funding. And in public debates about who should define the goals and measures of college writing, I fear that asserting that "being there matters" may not unsettle reform's appeals to standardization-for-competition, which now also claim to be "there" through "real-world" performance tasks for writing assessment. While the CLA appears to be moribund, I believe we will face its appeals again. In the rest of this chapter, I explore ways of performing our thereness—our local and contextual judgment—as a means of inviting public participation in authorizing professionalism. While of course this proposal is for a rhetoric of professionalism, my aim is to extend the capacity of our idealist style to invite public participation in authorizing professional judgment as responsiveness to public experiences with writing. In the following example, I describe a potential response to CLA-style "performance tasks," knowing that the next generation of college outcomes is likely to take up the CLA's appeal to real-world use. When we assert the value of being there, in other words, we will need to dramatize the "thereness" of our judgment in contrast with the "thereness" of reformers' judgment.

Thanks to *Academically Adrift*, the CLA has received considerable critical attention from scholars in composition and education. Much of that attention, however, has relied on a familiar rhetoric of professionalism. The claim that the CLA cannot be relied on because it is not statistically valid or reliable (Astin 2011; Haswell 2012; Kuh 2007) or fails to reflect discipline-specific knowledge (Banta and Pike 2007) enacts a familiar policy drama in which the debate is about getting the right methodology from the right people; another claim, that the CLA simply revives old decline narratives (Gunner 2012), enacts a drama in which the CLA is not to be taken seriously because it forwards the wrong purposes, and those wrong purposes can be attributed to the fact they come from the wrong people. While these responses engage us as professionals, they appear to be limited by their (agency- and purpose-centered) vocabulary as a means of reopening public inquiry into the worlds invoked by reformers. Calling out the CLA for ignoring disciplinary research has even less impact now that the CLA effectively creates its own reality through an extensive network of services: the "measurement science" of *CLA Testing*, the policy arm of *CLA Analysis*, the curriculum and pedagogy-development center of *CLA Education*, and a social science empirical unit, *CLA Research*

(Benjamin, Chun, and Jackson 2009). The critique of the CLA's failure to reflect disciplinary knowledge highlights the gap between testing and the various contexts of teaching and learning, but I anticipate the objection on the basis of agency falling back into idealist style: a call to assess disciplinary knowledge is a call to respect the professionalism of those who create it. In addition to exploiting the conventional terms of agency, agent, scene, or purpose, I propose inviting public attention to act—that of writing and of assessing a text according to criteria of value. While such an invitation is less directly engaged with the question of professionalism, it focuses on establishing public reference points otherwise unavailable amid debate.

The CLA claims to assess the critical thinking capacities students need to be competitive in the global marketplace. Because it features performance tasks, the argument goes, the CLA assesses student readiness for real writing situations. But these written performance tasks, which the CLA terms "make or break" an argument, rely on a contextualism that denies the socio-cognitive complexity of writing. For example, a forty-five-minute make-an-argument task presents students with the following prompt:

> You are the assistant to Pat Williams, the President of DynaTech, a company that makes precision electronic instruments and navigational equipment. Sally Evans, a member of DynaTech's sales force, recommended that DynaTech buy a small private plane (a SwiftAir 235) that she and other members of the sales force could use to visit customers. Pat was about to approve the purchase when there was an accident involving the SwiftAir 235. You are provided with the following documentation.
>
> - Newspaper articles about the incident
> - Federal Accident Report on in-flight breakups in single engine planes
> - Pat's email to you and Sally's email to Pat
> - Charts on SwiftAir's performance characteristics
> - Amateur Pilot article comparing SwiftAir 235 to similar planes
> - Pictures and description of SwiftAir Models 180 and 235
> - Please prepare a memo that addresses several questions, including what data support or refute the claim that the type

of wing on the SwiftAir 235 leads to more in-flight breakups, what other factors might have contributed to the accident and should be taken into account, and your overall recommendation about whether or not DynaTech should purchase the plane. (Klein et al. 2007, 7)

While the CLA argues that it "measures students' critical thinking, analytic reasoning, problem solving, and written communication skills with meaningful, holistic, complex tasks following in the tradition of the progressive education movement that can be traced back to the 1930s" (5), it is hard to see how this task appreciates the complexities of writing in an organizational setting. Would the writer of this performance task even be in a position to make a recommendation for this purchase? What makes this writer prepared to assess wing construction designs? And what ongoing conversations are in play within the company that would shape how the writer might frame his/her recommendations? These are questions that would arise from a realist focus on the act of composing in context but that are ignored in the CLA's task.

As I noted above, scholars have noted the CLA's refusal to acknowledge the disciplinarity of knowledge and writing, but their argument relies on the conventional appeals of bureaucratic and idealist style: the CLA's methods are flawed and they ignore disciplinary knowledge; they have selected the wrong means because they have the wrong people. To expand opportunities for public participation in this debate, I suggest we perform our inquiry into representative student acts of writing that take place in professional contexts. One source of these acts is our teaching. Like many others in composition, I frequently teach professional writing through partnerships in which advanced students assess the needs of local nonprofit groups and organizations. My students propose projects they believe can help organizations meet their writing needs, receive feedback on these proposals, revise their plans, and then develop documents and other media. The process of presentation, feedback, and revision continues throughout the semester. As Chris Anson and Lee Forsberg (1990) discuss in "Moving Beyond the

Academic Community," students' professional writing experiences tend to follow a series of transitions from expectations (what they thought "professional" writing would be) to struggle (what professional writing turns out to be) to accommodation (how they redefine professional writing and their roles as professional writers).

Yet like the Common Core professional development event discussed above, these professional touchstones are rarely accessible in public discussions of reform. Indeed, what we hear more of is the jeremiad issued by *Academically Adrift*: students are not learning what they need in order to do the work asked of them. "In an increasingly globalized competitive economy," authors Arum and Roksa (2011) argue, "the consequences of policy inattention are profound. Regardless of economic competitiveness, the future of a democratic society depends upon educating a generation of young adults who can think critically, reason deeply, and communicate effectively" (31). Instead of understanding that we teachers frequently bring students into contact with actual settings for professional writing, the reform discussion seems to repeat commonplaces about students' lack of readiness.

In one of his more memorable *New York Times* columns, economist Paul Krugman (2015) terms such phrases zombie ideas. Despite a lack of evidence, zombie ideas take on a life of their own through what appears to be the bad-faith recirculation of commonplaces. To counter the resonance of these zombie ideas in reform, we in composition have proposed telling our stories of possibility and potential. But as I've argued, these stories tend to follow a familiar pattern: students have potential, and reformers would see this *if* they'd measure writing the way professionals do. What this response does not appear to do, however, is invite public participation in assessing the adequacy of specific reforms, like the CLA's performance tasks, for measuring actual writing situations. My proposal here is for instructor performances of inquiry into student acts of writing that disclose the distance between reform assessments and professional experience. The purpose of this performance is to invite student inquiry into their own writing experiences. I'm assuming that many teachers have their own cases in mind; mine comes from a recent professional writing course.

A group of my students chose to work with a local nonprofit, a community bike shop (CBS). Conversations had been underway for at least a year between the CBS and student government at UNR about the possibility of developing a campus shop. The vision for such a shop was unique: it would continue to operate as a community shop, meaning that mechanics would be on hand to help students fix their own bikes and sell consumable parts. But the campus shop would not be a conventional retail operation. At first, my students were excited. They liked the idea of a community shop keeping cycling affordable for students, and the educational element—learning how to fix their own bikes—was attractive. In Anson and Forsberg's terms, my students were expecting to enter the writing situation, provide their recommendations, and watch the project move forward.

But then students began researching other universities' shops. These other shops operated on different models: some incorporated the CBS approach while others went fully commercial. My students began emailing with questions: how can we tell the CBS that we don't see their vision as viable in this particular context? In an early draft of their documents, my students offered what I considered to be tone-deaf recommendations: they suggested to the CBS that they should not pursue the aim they had identified and instead try another approach. The only way to establish a shop on campus, they argued, was by adopting a retail model. At this stage, my students were frustrated. They could not see how to "make recommendations" to the CBS when their research suggested the shop's vision was not viable. In Anson and Forsberg's terms, my students were struggling with the constraints of an actual writing situation.

However, using my feedback, they began to construct a different picture of their role in professional writing. They were newcomers to an existing setting: the CBS is ten years old and financially stable. UNR is growing and seeking to transform transportation on campus. They recognized that other campus models might not predict all possibilities here. And so they refashioned their "recommendations": they named the aims of the CBS, foregrounded the issues they explored, and then presented their findings not as proposals for action but as important considerations for stakeholders. In the end, my students' report encouraged both the CBS and student organizations at UNR to continue talking about how they might address what seemed like roadblocks in the process. Although some students on this team remained unhappy, the remaining members of the team recognized that they were learning how to work within constraints—not to give recommendations but to provide information leaders needed to make important decisions. Some of the students, in their end-of-semester reflections, recognized that they were making recommendations in their choices of sources and in their framing of the issue. In Anson and Forsberg's terms, my students had begun the process of "accommodation."

I recount this case to show how students' acts of writing can disclose not only the agency of critical thinking ("make or break an argument") but also the range of agents, agencies, scenes, and purposes at play in a writing situation. That is, acts of writing reveal the complexity of rhetorical judgment. The goal of forwarding our inquiry into representative acts would not be simply to displace the CLA's assessment, although that is obviously an appealing aim. Rather, an additional goal would be to make possible a public assessment of the CLA's claims to represent what students learn and what students need to do. It's hard to imagine students or administrators affirming the "thereness" of the CLA's performance tasks alongside the experience of writing for a real audience, with real constraints.

Another drama is similar to the one suggested above, but it compares writing taught in advanced disciplinary contexts to the testing scenario. Such an approach may sound like a conventional appeal to idealist style: that is, we would point to the advanced disciplinary context as an example with the right agency delivered by the right agents while discounting the testing context as the wrong agency delivered by the wrong agents.

But showing an act of teaching writing does not have to collapse immediately into idealist style; it can also disclose the broader set of factors involved in disciplinary-professional participation. For example, above I argued that the make-an-argument performance task reduces the socio-cognitive complexity of writing to a performance of pseudo-competence. To bring out how teachers attempt to address this complexity, I suggest focusing on an act of teaching, such as staging and responding to writing assignments.

Like many other writing teachers, I organize my professional writing courses around projects that require students to learn the unstated discourse conventions of their writing situations. The process of inquiring into an office's or an organization's public communication challenges groups of students to fill out their picture of the genre and constraints of a writing situation. Above I described the process through which my students came to write "for" local nonprofit groups and organizations.[1] I place quotes around "for" because the task of learning to write was not as clear as the "client project" assignment suggested. Following Anson and Forsberg, I staged out the writing process to uncover the complexity of writing for a particular audience (Anson and Forsberg 1990). This process challenged my students to develop what Jamie MacKinnon (1998) calls "rhetorical maturity." Such maturity, MacKinnon suggests, is based on knowledge gained through the experience of inquiry. What is the social and organizational context? What is an appropriate writing process, given this context? What is an appropriate written product, given the needs of readers in this context? And what attitudes and beliefs about writing make sense, given the experience of professional writing?

To answer these questions, my students moved through phases of expectation, struggle, and accommodation. As I noted, some students persisted in believing that they could simply create written products "for" their "clients." But most of my students gained perspective on the questions MacKinnon poses. In the social and organizational context of the CBS, students were *not* in a position to recommend a retail model. In fact, the shop had succeeded *because* they were not a retail outfit: there are plenty commercial shops in the area, and the CBS serves people who can't afford or don't want to shop retail. My students realized this eventually, but only after pursuing the image of a writing process they'd developed before entering the class. To write for a client, they believed, means being assigned a task, researching peer organizations, and making a recommendation. When this process was interrupted by feedback from the CBS, students were frustrated: they felt like they were being asked to start over with a new perspective. And they were. But no matter how many times I explained that the point of professional writing is to understand clients' needs, students persisted in believing that writing happens in a straight line. It was only when they experienced the disjunction between their process and the situation that they began to adopt a different way of producing documents: listening, asking questions, proposing, revising—all before drafting.

Students also learned about an appropriate written product for the situation and the process. Students read models of proposals but still struggled to write in a reader-centered format. It was only when members of the CBS read the proposal that students began to experience the need for common professional writing document elements like an executive summary, background, findings, recommendations, and so on. And, it was only at this point that my earlier cautions to the group about tone and stance became live considerations: members of the organization asked students what they might do, despite students' resistance to the idea of a CBS. Finally, through this process, students described a change in their attitudes and beliefs about writing. Yes, they were still frustrated by the mismatch between their expectations and their experience, but in their end-of-course reflections, students also recognized their experiences as valuable for their future work as writers. As one of my students wrote,

> This project was a good way to understand how working with a client is different from working on a project for a teacher. When [we] began brainstorming before discussing the project with our client, we set ourselves behind in schedule by already affirming where we wanted to go in this project. If we had used this time

in the beginning to meet with our client and understand exactly what they wanted and in which direct to go, we may have had more time to devote to the new direction of the project. As it was, we did not have as much time left to truly meet the needs that they had because of our early brainstorming . . . If we had met with our client earlier and then kept up with consistent contact and feedback with our client, then we may have been able to produce a product that was better received.

To approach the task of professional writing successfully, this student had to re-orient her conception of writing process. Now compare my class's "performance task" to the "break-an-argument" prompt from the CLA:

> The University of Claria is generally considered one of the best universities in the world because of its instructors' reputation, which is based primarily on the extensive research and publishing record of certain faculty members. In addition, several faculty members are internationally renowned as leaders in their fields. For example, many of the English Department's faculty members are regularly invited to teach at universities in other countries. Furthermore, two recent graduates of the physics department have gone on to become candidates for the Nobel Prize in Physics. And 75 percent of the students are able to find employment after graduating. Therefore, because of the reputation of its faculty, the University of Claria should be the obvious choice for anyone seeking a quality education. (Klein et al. 2007, 8)

Students responding to this prompt are not asked to consider the questions listed above: what is the social and organizational context in which my report will be read? For this reason, it does not require a process of inquiry and revision, only a brief timed writing performance. And, given this lack of process, the CLA does not challenge students to find out what kinds of written products would serve the needs of readers in this situation. It is no wonder that students writing for this prompt would develop the belief that professional writing simply means make or break an argument.

Performing our inquiry into acts of teaching professional writing can invite students to attend to differences between the context of the test and the context of actual organizations. Rather than issuing a make or break scenario, teachers of

professional writing encourage students to reflect on their judgment while learning how to work within (and perhaps against
the grain of) discourse communities. The goal of performing
our inquiry into teaching acts would not be just to forward the
right agency or the right agents but to make professional judgment publicly accessible for inquiry. This judgment encompasses a range of factors (agent, scene, agency, purpose) in a
single act and highlights the difference between actual contexts
for writing and the stipulated context of the CLA's performance
task. It is hard to imagine that anyone who values "professional"
writing or "career-readiness" would choose reform's acts of
teaching over those practiced within composition.

Certainly, the CLA's response to this critique and others is
that they're simply measuring student outcomes to know what
needs improvement. And this argument has enabled the CLA
to deflect many of our objections to the standardization and
marketization of writing expertise. But comparisons between
the CLA's tasks and actual classroom tasks may help our students and our publics ask whose approach is more adequate
for responding to public experiences with writing. Inviting
our students to inquire into their experiences can dramatize
the grounds of our professional writing, and we can circulate our students' inquiry more broadly to create pressure on
public officials who are investing in CLA. As I acknowledged
in chapter 1, students are not yet inquiring critically into
the "discourse of student need" as a warrant for neoliberal
standardization. But these moments of professional writing
practice suggest opportunities for student protests to render
reform's stock appeals to competition, efficiency, and testing-
accountability suddenly empty. An alternate realist style offers
us a starting point, if only for a moment, to unsettle the commonplaces of reform.

ARTFULNESS FOR SCALING UP

If being there offers a promising method of going public, how
might we extend the potential of thereness to sponsor both

local and broader public engagement? The problem of going public—scaling down to the local and scaling up to policy debate—relies on what Dewey calls "artfulness." In chapter 3, I discussed artfulness in critique, but here I am concerned with artfulness in storytelling. In *Art as Experience*, Dewey (1935) argues that art needs to create experiences of inquiry: "the question for the critic is the adequacy of form to matter, and thus of the presence or absence of any particular form. The value of experience is not only in the ideals it reveals, but in its power to disclose many ideals, a power more germinal and more significant than any revealed ideal, since it includes them in its stride, shatters and remakes them" (322). In this light, accounts of "being there" can invite public audiences into what Dewey called "aesthetic experiences," or as Scott Stroud puts it, "moments when audiences reflect on a situation with the goal of settling a problem" (Stroud 2011, 37). Thus, stories of student success in basic writing courses, or of judgment in context providing fully rounded assessments of learning, *can* reveal the limits of reform's realist style to reflect the range of contexts, experiences, and purposes associated with literacy education.

But such stories are common. What separates artful storytelling from what Dewey (1927) calls "conventionalized" communication (168)? In light of the experiences described above, what might allow storytelling to break with conventionality? The pragmatic tradition suggests an approach. For Stroud (2011), an activity is artful based on the attention one gives to a situation (43). "Nonartful activity," on the other hand, "stems from an orientation that separates the present qua means from the end to be accomplished and subordinates the former to the latter." In the context of this chapter, Stroud's argument suggests that artful storytelling about reform attends to the specifics of the teaching, learning, and assessing situation without resolving too quickly to the contested ambiguities of the debate—how the scene, agency, agent, and purpose of education should be defined.

As this chapter illustrates, artfulness is difficult: being there and storytelling would seem like the very enactment of artfulness in that they attend to the need for judgment in context. But as I have suggested, amid the stalemates of debate, the assertion of thereness tends to collapse into an agency, a policy means, that can be displaced by other agencies. As a rhetoric of professionalism, an agency alone—whether it favors pluralization or standardization—provides a narrow zone of recalcitrance, or a scant range of possible ways to sponsor public inquiry into and critique of reform.[2] Likewise, telling stories would seem to enact artfulness in the way that the drama of local experience—disclosing how an agency affects agents, and how agents are enabled or prevented from fulfilling shared purposes—would appear to spur on the dialectic of debate that can mature perspectives on reform. But storytelling in itself does not innovate on the ways that we go public in the face of debate; even the agency of disciplinary research collapses to agents, and the stories intended to reopen dialectic amount to pleas for one set of agents over another.

My argument here, in light of these stalemates of debate, is that artfulness attends to the situation of judgment—the acts of teaching, learning, and assessment. The goal of art, as Dewey describes it, is to create aesthetic experiences in which audiences reconsider their terms and perspectives in light of their experiences. This description may sound like compositionists pursuing artfulness must always unsettle conventionalized communication and never resolve their arguments to idealist style, but that is not my argument. For teachers, scholars, and administrators seeking to go public, artfulness does *not* provide a full break from the central commonplace of professionalism, idealist style. When we scale up by circulating accounts of inquiry, we return, eventually, to idealist style. Rather than offering a break with idealist style, artfulness works from other starting points in discussion—here, acts. One way to practice artfulness is to enact an alternate realist style that foregrounds the need for inquiry and expands from acts to the contentious definitions of purpose, agents, agency, and scene. An alternate realist style extends the drama as it moves from acts to questions of agents and of professional standing.

If an alternate realist style eventually falls back into idealist style, what's the point of the innovation I propose? Given our reliance on idealist style, our efforts at going public will always resolve to the agent as the locus of expertise and judgment. But, efforts to go public can enact idealist style in a variety of ways. An inquiry-driven realist style is a conscious effort to locate professional judgment in the publicly accessible grounds of acts. Moreover, an alternate realist style invites our publics' participation in the process of defining the contexts of teaching and learning. If going public on the basis of the definition of the scene is unartful—that is, if saying "the world is diverse rather than a single scene of competition" does not sponsor local public inquiry—then we need to develop other grounds on which to highlight the inadequacy of reform to reflect public experience. The same goes for our appeals to agents (professionals, not reformers), agency (pluralistic, not standardized), and purpose (democratic, not competition). If going public is to break up conventionalized communication and "calcified" perspectives (Burke 1972, 19), it needs to expand the areas of potential resistance in debate. In the present debates, the case for professionalism, with its appeals to agents, purpose, scene, and agency, appears to do little to unsettle the realist drama of reform. An alternate realist style, focused on inquiry into acts, may provide more publicly accessible grounds for affirming professional standing.

These grounds attract the scholars who go public via public engagement. In response to the stalemates of the debate, the innovation of public engagement offers not only idealist, materialist, pragmatic, or mystical styles (Burke 1984a, 128–31). Rather, these scholars suggest a realist style of inquiry that points to the need for alternate educational purposes, scenes, agencies, and agents. In short, public engagement is concerned with the pragmatic project of sponsoring a democratic culture of critical inquiry as well as the conventional project of defending professional standing. Whereas scholars calling for reframing see the exigency of deprofessionalization and seek to bring about a new conversation by expanding the dominant discourse of reform, and scholars calling for a rhetoric of bureaucracy seek to expand the discourse of management, scholars focused on public engagement turn away, in part, from professional style in an effort to build democratic experiences at the level of means as well as ends. Public engagement enacts a form of antiprofessionalism by dramatizing our inquiry into acts and our discovery of multiple purposes, agents, agencies, and scenes; circulating accounts of this inquiry to sponsor parallel efforts in other local contexts; and inviting public assessments of professional judgment based on the experience of inquiry in local contexts.

As a rhetorical enactment of pragmatism, public engagement offers not only a model of phronesis but also a broader rhetorical education for composition teachers and scholars. While the case for public engagement is certainly concerned with institutional and professional publics, it also envisions circulation among community, regional, and national publics. For these publics, there are conventional rhetorics of professionalism but also more dissent- and inquiry-based rhetorics of expertise. And, in these rhetorical performances, there are not only the possibilities of professional self-defense but also those of public-professional cooperation and collaboration. These are the possibilities I believe can be served by an alternate realist style. But as I explore in the next chapter, the antiprofessionalism implicit in such a style both meets and challenges our commitments to ethical public representation.

NOTES

1. Following Thomas Deans's model of "writing for," my students produced mostly workplace documents for local organizations.

2. Lawrence Prelli, Floyd Anderson, and Matthew Althouse define "zones of recalcitrance" in the following terms (Prelli, Anderson, and Althouse 2011). "When critics bring alternative perspectives into contact and disclose how meanings and 'realities' revealed by the terms of one perspective remain concealed by the terms of others they are pointing out what we might call 'zones of recalcitrance.' When applied to hegemonic discourses, counter-statements that evoke incongruous points of view create zones of recalcitrance that, at least partially, open the universe of discourse by enabling expression of a wider range of voices that—through

revising, reshaping, rephrasing, and correcting—could ultimately yield a more mature, more encompassing, and less reductive orientation toward a situation" (116–17). My argument here is that composition's idealist style of professionalism opens a narrow zone of recalcitrance in contemporary reform debate.

Chapter 5
AN ETHICS OF DISSENT

While at the 2015 CCCC, I attended a panel on large-scale standardized writing assessments.[1] In their presentations, Norbert Elliot, Mya Poe, and David Slomp described how we can understand the consequences of these assessments for students' access to opportunity. When conventional assessment practices disproportionately place students of color in basic writing courses, the presenters suggested, we should validate these practices using the legal lens of disparate impact analysis. Based on this analysis, we can begin to envision alternate assessment practices better suited to upholding the constitutionally protected values of fairness and ethics.

In his conclusion to the panel, Bob Broad situated these aims within the political economy of contemporary reform. We who work in writing assessment, Broad argued, offer more than expertise. Rather, we provide contextual judgment with attention to the democratic consequences of our expertise. Our professional inquiry serves public goods. Large-scale assessments, on the other hand, serve largely private goods. While the ETS competes successfully in the assessment marketplace, it fails to account for fairness and civil rights. Thus, large-scale testing hardly offers what we'd consider an expertise adequate to higher education's democratic aims. But this shortcoming is not the ETS' central concern. To underscore this last point, Broad invoked Upton Sinclair's lament that "it is difficult to get a man to understand something when his salary depends on his not understanding it."

With this argument, Broad was not going public in the sense I've described. Still, the terms of his critique invited us in the

DOI: 10.7330/9781607326540.c005

audience to anticipate a public response to our concerns with large-scale testing. Drawing forceful contrasts between the public and private goods of assessment, Broad suggested, *should* help us affirm professionalism as a more ethical social logic than bureaucracy or markets. Even when testing companies refuse to engage our critical perspectives, our critiques are still valuable because they can invite our local publics, and particularly our students, to inquire into the tests' capacity to serve public goods. If these local inquiries can scale up to the national scene of reform, our research, teaching, and administration can demonstrably improve what Peter Mortensen (1998) calls "the prospects of literacy in democratic culture" (182).

In his response to the panel, however, Doug Baldwin of the Educational Testing Service undercut this hope for going public. Rather than acknowledging the ethical limits of corporate testing, Baldwin accused writing assessment professionals of the same blindness Sinclair described. Teachers, scholars, and administrators, he argued, also draw a salary, and for that reason, *they* stubbornly deny the need for large-scale assessments. This panel's concern with ethics, then, can be understood as a pretense for professionals seeking to preserve their monopoly on expertise. The proper public response to concerns with social justice, Baldwin implied, is to demand consumer choice among a broader range of service providers. *That* would be public engagement. Judging by the lack of questions for Baldwin when he finished speaking, no one in the audience quite knew how to respond to the insinuation of professional malfeasance. But Broad fidgeted in his chair, clearly anxious to speak, and when he did, he said what I believe many in the room were thinking. "With respect to the members of the panel," Broad said carefully, "I think that a public servant is different from a corporation." And then the panel ended.

This moment dramatizes the specter I've invoked throughout this book: what happens when our claim to serve democratic public goods is read as just another market-share seeking rhetoric? Granted, Baldwin's retort—essentially, "you're competitors, too"—may not indicate a broader public reading. But responses like Baldwin's are powerful because they reorient reform discussion to the plane of the economic, where we are challenged, again and again, to defend professionalism against competing social logics. If we don't offer the standardization of bureaucracy or the competition of markets, what *do* we offer? To answer this question, Broad invoked the methodology of disparate impact analysis (Poe et al. 2014): as professionals, we inquire into the local consequences of assessment practice, and based on this inquiry, we follow through on a democratic ethics of public representation. But as the 2015 CCCC anecdote suggests, this professional claim to serve the public good still confronts the rhetorical constraints endemic to reform debate. Under these constraints, Broad's forceful contrast between public and private goods fell back into the realist-idealist style stalemate, and the discussion collapsed into a contest between closed and open markets of expertise.

Still, the argument of this book is that we can extend Broad's response to reform. We offer expertise for the public good, yes, but not only via the reassertion of professionalism as the bulwark of democracy. Going public can also perform our professional inquiry into local acts of assessment as a means of inviting our publics' inquiry into these assessments' consequences. We can then circulate accounts of this inquiry with the aim of sponsoring broader public participation in reform debate, participation that can potentially authorize the publicness of our judgment. Indeed, disparate impact analysis suggests cases for professional inquiry that, in the spirit of Chris Gallagher's (2011) "being there," return the scene of assessment to the local. An alternate realist style may provide a means of scaling up from local consequences to the broader debate over assessment in the political economy of reform. When our professional standing is discounted as mere market share-seeking, in other words, we may wager on the antiprofessionalism of public participation as an alternate means of advancing professional values.

In the meantime, however, we frequently find ourselves in the same situation as Broad, forced to articulate the public good of our professionalism on the spot. This exigency reminds us that while pragmatic inquiry may offer a resource for antiprofessional rhetorical innovation, the practice of going public pulls us back to conventional professional style. In philosopher Colin Koopman's (2009) terms, we still find ourselves "getting through" (2) one situation after another (see chapter 2). So, while this book has pointed toward an alternate means of going public, it also seeks to appreciate the pragmatic innovations of bureaucracy, reframing, and being there. These innovations are essential, especially when partisans like Baldwin do their best to resituate discussion on the plane of the economic. Idealist style was what I could manage, for example, in my response to representatives of Smarter Balanced (chapter 4). I didn't have an antiprofessional drama to enact at that moment, and even if I had, I would have needed time to develop materials, practices, channels, and even dispositions for this work. There is a lot to do and try before an alternate realist style is viable for going public.

This chapter does not address all of these concerns but it begins to qualify the potential of an alternate realist style for going public. What does it mean for us in composition to commit to dissent-building? To circulating representations of our publics' experiences beyond our professional spheres? To opening our rhetoric of professionalism to inquiry? While these questions highlight the challenges of an alternate pragmatism for going public, I argue that they also point toward opportunities to forge new relationships with our publics, relationships oriented more toward what John Trimbur (2011) terms "solidarity" than "service." Even though "professional practices and discourses typically represent the dispossessed as a client population in need of the intervention of expert benefactors," Trimbur argues, "the political valence and cultural meaning of professional work nonetheless cannot be guaranteed in advance as an accommodation to the dominant culture and its division of specialists and laypeople. Professional expertise . . . can also articulate a sense of solidarity with the aspirations and purposes of the dispossessed" (28–29). Admittedly, the solidarity I am describing is marked by differences in power, and as professionals, we stand to benefit differently from public engagement than, say, our basic writing students might. But I find in an alternate pragmatism a promising ethics of public representation. In the rest of this chapter, I elaborate this ethics and contend with the complexity of going public in an alternate mode.

FROM THE EXPERIENCE OF INQUIRY
TO A RHETORIC OF INQUIRY

This book's anecdotes dramatize a familiar process. Working within our field, we innovate on our defenses of professionalism. We then rehearse these innovations in proto-public venues to discover the limits of our publicity. Based on this inquiry, we attempt alternate innovations: in pragmatic terms, we seek better ways of attending to consequences, meliorating problematic situations, and sponsoring public engagement. However, as I have argued, our rhetorical innovations both enable and hamstring our pragmatic inquiry. Those innovations best suited to defending professionalism tend to work against the antiprofessionalism that enables democratic public formation. Meanwhile, those innovations best suited to public engagement tend to undermine the work of reasserting professionalism.

The tension between professionalism and antiprofessionalism is deep, and recovering an alternate pragmatism does not resolve composition's discussion about how we should innovate on going public. In fact, this book's efforts may calcify our discussion if they only affirm the potential of antiprofessionalism to advance professional values. Certainly, I believe that circulating student inquiry into reform proposals for cutting basic writing, implementing machine scoring, and standardizing outcomes assessments *can* invite broader public participation in assessing our professional judgment. And, I believe that that such participation can authorize our professionalism as responsiveness to public experience. But given the probabilistic nature of these beliefs, I would like to emphasize a shorter-term potentiality. Even if antiprofessional analysis and innovation ultimately fall short as defenses of our professional standing, these efforts still offer us a compensatory value in the present:

they help us learn from what Robert Hariman (1989, 229) calls professional rhetorical failure. Following in the tradition of a rhetoric of inquiry, an alternate realist style calls attention to the performances through which we attempt to claim and defend our expert standing (218). Certainly, our professional rhetorical failures are vexing, but inquiry into them can offer a unique reward: it can disclose alternate logics and rhetorical styles overshadowed by our professional concern with self-preservation.

Admittedly, this critical reward may be cold comfort. As Hariman argues, professional scholars are socialized to engage in spatialization, or rhetorically performing as if their knowledge is separate from power (218). Hariman illustrates spatialization through the example of economists whose perspectives on policy are frequently "too limited to be powerful" (219) in public debate. As professionals, however, economists must forward their views in this carefully disciplined manner to avoid being "discredited as being unlearned or popular or partisan or eccentric or radical or utopian." Like the economists of Hariman's example, we in composition have grown frustrated with the failures of our professional rhetorical performances when going public. In response to these failures, we have developed the innovations of bureaucracy, reframing, and public engagement. Yet these innovations are rhetorically limited by our concerns with preserving professionalism. We have a commitment to inquiry that leads us beyond our commonplaces, and yet we recognize the political-economic costs of innovating on those commonplaces. We may open our rhetoric of professionalism to a broader range of styles and publics, but such a reopening may diminish the standing that gives us the opportunity to innovate in the first place. Idealist style is durable for a reason.

Still, Hariman's response to this dilemma is instructive. Rather than designate a rhetoric of inquiry suitable for critical analysis within the field and a conventional professional style suitable for going public, he envisions the rhetoric of inquiry expanding the boundaries of our professionalism by "excavat[ing] the knowledges interned at the emergence of the university culture" (223). Given rhetoric's adversarial relationship with professional knowledge (224), Hariman goads scholars to envision models of communication relationships outside the norms of "expertise, productivity, and social control." Rather than contributing to the disciplining of professionalism, Hariman argues, "the rhetoric of inquiry should be used as a means for the recovery of rhetoric, and especially those versions of the rhetorical tradition squelched by professionalism" (226). We should not only recover antiprofessional modes of argument, in other words, but also enact these modes in our critiques of professional style. We should reopen our rhetoric of professionalism to expand its sociological reach.

Here the aims of an alternate realist style align with the aims of a rhetoric of inquiry. Based on this consonance, an alternate realist style would appear to offer a meeting ground between the critical and productive traditions in rhetoric and composition. Yet my goal in forwarding an alternate standard of rhetorical judgment is not to call for antiprofessionalism as the new rhetoric of professionalism in composition. Hariman similarly tempers hopes for a shared standard, arguing that a rhetoric of inquiry should not be interpreted as a reliable source of a profession's politics. A rhetoric of inquiry, he cautions, "may create as many problems as it solves" (229). Such a caution hardly needs elaboration in composition: the tactics of antiprofessionalism I have proposed may resonate with our values of critical inquiry and public engagement, but such tactics may never amount to an effective defense of professional judgment. Rather, the reward of a rhetoric of inquiry is that it helps us maintain an adjacency to the conventions of our own profession. This is my aim with a *partial* embrace of antiprofessionalism. The tactic of scaling down to scale up is, as Hariman puts it, "more than a methodological analysis of expert discourse" (229). It is an alternate rhetorical performance, a bid for inquiry, both inside and outside the field.

Admittedly, this bid is not entirely conciliatory. Much of my argument here has been for expanding our style in the direction of dissent. Like what communication rhetorician Kevin Michael DeLuca (1999, 52) calls image events, an alternate realist style works more through disidentification than through identification. The circulation of local inquiry seeks play on what DeLuca and Jennifer Peeples call "public screens" (DeLuca and Peeples 2002, 128), the tightly controlled messaging venues of corporate-political power.[2] Unsurprisingly, the quality of discussion available on these screens is problematic. As DeLuca and Peeples put it, the public screen tends to value dissemination as much as dialogue (130). To embrace the conventions of this setting, we professionals would enter the agon of images. That is, rather than offering expert critique as a corrective to the spectacles of publicity staged by reform groups, going public would work through spectacle (133–34). This quality of the public screen especially resonates with an alternate realist style. For DeLuca and Peeples, image events represent "visual philosophical-rhetorical mind bombs that expand the universe of thinkable thoughts" (136). When critics show a situation, especially one intended to sponsor public recalcitrance, an image event "participates in order to be aired—it is brief, visual, dramatic, and emotional. It punctures to punctuate, to interrupt the flow, to give pause. It punctures by making the mundane malevolent, the familiar fantastic" (145). Similarly, the aim of circulating accounts of students' local inquiry into the elimination of basic writing (chapter 2), the implementation of machine scoring (chapter 3), and the use of standardized outcomes assessment (chapter 4) is to sponsor public dissent that can unsettle the commonplace of reform, standardization-for-competition-for-democracy. The hope of such dissent-building is that its critical publicity can help us accomplish what professionalism has not.

My bid to reopen dialectic within composition, in other words, recognizes the capacity of outsider innovation to advance insider values. In this way, an alternate realist style follows in the tradition established by the innovations of bureaucracy, reframing, and public engagement. I envision professionalism as enriched by its rhetorical and sociological expansion. But such expansion also has likely consequences of its own. When we commit to sponsoring and circulating the antiprofessional energy of local inquiry, we recast our role in representing our publics. Here Susan Wells's (1996) question—"what do we want from public writing?"—can be put to our purposes for going public. What do we professionals want from circulating our publics' dissent? Our working answer to this question has been that, in Peter Mortensen's (1998) words, we believe that our "teaching, researching, and theorizing can clarify and even improve the prospects of literacy in democratic culture" (182). We share what we consider to be more ethical representations of public experience than those offered by reform, and we hope that these representations will invite critical public participation that can affirm our judgment. An alternate realist style, however, shifts our stance from *sharing* representations to *sponsoring* public critique. What we want from dissent is to improve the publicness of policy. Thus, we turn our attention to fostering critical public participation and circulating images that dramatize this participation.

In constructing image events to circulate on the public screens of reform, however, we stylize public experience. We position ourselves as curators of public experience out of a faith that our professionalism will be authorized as publicness. As Wells (1996) points out, this positioning is ethically ambiguous: just as political candidates may select and present citizen voices as a sort of "inartistic proof" (329) in support of policies, we have the potential to "ventriloquize" (330) public inquiry for defending our own professional standing. Like reformers, we who enact an alternate realist drama disavow, to some degree, our concerns with professionalism. We justify this disavowal on the grounds that we foreground acts of writing not as a reason to *close* debate but as reason to *reopen* and *expand* debate. Such a justification may be persuasive to us, but as Wells notes, this too is a familiar political gesture in which candidates deny seeking a particular policy goal but embrace the notions of reopening public discussion, allowing more people to have a fair say on the issue, and letting the best idea win (329). For us as professionals, of course, there's little mystery about the purpose of enacting an alternate realist style: it's a means of generating dissensus when reform's arguments command great certainty.

So, an alternate realist style, ethical as it may be in its aims for contextual representations of literacy, is selective about how fully it acknowledges the purposes of its rhetorical performances. Despite the rationale I have developed in this book—that public participation can form a more public professionalism—public inquiry into reform *may* benefit us more concretely than it benefits our local publics. This possibility sits uneasily with Jeffrey Grabill's (2007, 16) argument that "the value of any contemporary rhetorical art is how useful it (and we) can be for others." In the Deweyan tradition, professionals sponsoring public inquiry into issues of shared concern *are* useful, but critical public inquiry into K–16 reform may not be the most pressing "use" for parents or students. By contrast, more fully antiprofessional community literacy projects—like Lorraine Higgins and Lisa Brush's account of their work with mothers to craft public narratives of their experiences with welfare—suggest a clearer definition of who the subordinated public is, who benefits from this collaboration, and how the collaboration might work against the internal exclusions of political debate (Higgins and Brush 2006).

If an ethics of dissent is ambiguous, what makes it worth the trouble? The value of such an ethics, I believe, is that it recognizes the public screens of national reform as opportunities for sponsoring and circulating the energy of local counterpublicity. In calling for professionals to perform our inquiry into acts of teaching and learning and then circulate accounts of local inquiry, I am recognizing the potential for public dissent to circulate outside our conventional professional channels. The contemporary reform scene would suggest that these channels are largely closed: we offer our critical feedback on efforts like the Common Core, the Collegiate Learning Assessment, and Complete College America, and this feedback is ignored by state leaders, systems of higher education, and institution-level administrators. To be sure, the reframing work of the AAC&U stands as a counterexample to this trend. The challenge of responding to the CLA appears now to have been the challenge of redirecting calls for assessment in higher education.

But we are certain to face future reforms that claim to offer not only better outcomes but also a more democratic form of literacy education expertise. Anticipating this challenge leads me to read the closing of conventional professional channels as the opening of alternate channels. Following Catherine Chaput (2010) and Jenny Edbauer (2005) in their discussions of rhetorical circulation, I read "the local" of teaching, learning, and assessment as promising sites on an otherwise calcified political-economic network. Particularly, I recognize the local as a site of potential connectivity between professionals and our publics that creates a certain energy of being together (Chaput 2010, 7–8). There is an "intensity" (Edbauer 2005) possible in the gathering of a local public. The presence of local realities—the scenes, agencies, agents, and purposes of literacy education disclosed through inquiry into acts—can be great in the context of experience, great enough to sponsor the kind of inquiry rarely experienced in national debate. This was the togetherness I experienced, if only momentarily, in conversations with K–12 parents, with my student Anthony, and with my professional writing students.

A move toward circulating dissenting public inquiry would also recognize the limits of managerial and professional rhetorics for public engagement in the contemporary reform scene. While these means of going public can serve writing professionals well, the historical shift toward marketizing expertise has weakened them both. The rhetoric and sociology of professionalism are being disrupted in the present moment, a moment Chaput (2010) describes as "economic neoliberalism mov[ing] from situation to situation, disregarding spatial boundaries between the political, economic, and cultural realms as well as their attendant modes of persuasion, wearing away at the rhetorical linkages between appropriate discursive choices and agentive power" (2–3). This trend enables what I have called the displacement of idealist style (and of our professional standing) by calls for standardization-for-competition-for-democracy. While our conventional rhetorics of professionalism are "infected" (Edbauer 2005, 14) with certain social energies,

these energies do not appear to have sponsored public recalcitrance amid the political economy of reform.

My argument here, then, is that sponsoring public dissent
represents an ethical innovation for advancing the aims of professionalism. With this judgment, I am claiming a *partial* resolution to the problem Carolyn Miller (2010) calls "naming the
tools." In efforts to educate their publics, Miller notes, rhetorical
critics typically explain how dominant perspectives invite public
identification. Critics name the tools. Yet these critical analyses,
Miller argues, often fail as public engagement: they tend not to
sponsor public participation beyond suspicion of power. Self-
denying rhetorical performances, on the other hand, often succeed politically. Like realist or idealist style, these performances
hide their status as a rhetoric and successfully induce public
cooperation, but these performances neglect the public project
of building social trust. These trends leave Miller to conclude
that "rhetoric, it seems, must deny itself to succeed" (20). What
then, Miller asks, "can rhetoric's public role be under these
conditions?...What happens if we teach students to name—and
master—the tools? Can rhetoric be useful or powerful if it is
revealed—both as a practice and as a discipline?" (30–31).

Although Miller discusses the public work of rhetoric without reference to reform, her questions frame the central issue
of this book. To enact composition's conventional rhetoric of
professionalism, we deny our tools of idealist style. Such a denial
recognizes that idealist style can serve as a political-economic
anti-rhetoric in which one must have experts to get expertise. In contemporary reform debates, however, realist style
performs an even more absolute anti-rhetoric: if world, then
competition, and if competition, then democracy. To counter
this anti-rhetoric, it would seem, going public should name
the tools of reform in order to sponsor critical public inquiry
into invocations like "competitiveness." But we already name
reform's tools through critique; we already know that reform's
invocations of global competition narrow public debate about
literacy education to the scope of neoliberal rationality. The
aim of an alternate realist style is to fashion a performance that

innovates on the familiar ways through which we deny the tools of our professionalism—through appeals to democratic purpose, to the diverse scenes of teaching and learning, and to the agencies of disciplinary research. In Miller's terms, I forward a denial of professionalism's tools that aims to sponsor publics' desires to name reform's tools. An alternate realist style invites our local publics to inquire into acts of teaching, learning, and assessment. Rather than arguing that "the purpose of literacy education is democratic preparation," an alternate realist style chooses acts that may disclose the realities (scenes, agents, agencies, purposes) typically marginalized by reform. The aim of foregrounding this broader range of terms and perspectives is to unsettle realist style and restart a broader dialectic among participants in debate.

This aim reflects both small and big hopes for rhetoric. While inviting local inquiry is one thing, scaling up public participation is another. Miller is cautious about such big hopes, urging "a realistic attenuation of our hopes for what it is that rhetoric can achieve in public, both in terms of its status as a discipline and in terms of its capabilities to promote the public good" (33). Rather than calling for a "global or programmatic" effort to build a rhetoric that "helps build social trust," Miller encourages us to "risk" going public "one situation at a time." This conclusion parallels the spirit of pragmatic experimentalism I have emphasized in the previous chapters. Certainly, composition's rhetoric of professionalism is profoundly constrained. But these constraints do not dictate that we suspend our search for a public rhetoric of professionalism; on the contrary, a pragmatic inquiry stance would encourage us to consider constraining factors as potential resources for inquiry. So, while I heed Miller's caution, I also recognize in it a thread of opportunity. Scaling down *can* build the conditions for scaling up.

Still, this potential is uncertain, and in turning away from what Margaret Marshall (2004, 150) terms "the position and language of professionalism," we may open ourselves to new forms of scrutiny. As Marshall argues, locating literacy education among the professions has allowed teachers, scholars, and administrators to counter claims of teaching as "women's work" (19–20) and of composition as a feminized practice (150). Just as contemporary reform's economic framing of expertise has rendered our professionalism vulnerable to marketization, a shift toward antiprofessional modes of going public may invite gendered re-assessments of composition professionals' hard-won standing. In light of these potential consequences, I recognize the need for idealist style. Yet I also note, as Marshall observes, that when reforms call for the "professionalization" of teachers, these reforms often *undermine* teachers' standing as those specially "prepared to make informed, intelligent judgments appropriate for the given situation" (166). Indeed, "professionalization" under contemporary K–16 reform frequently entails the standardization and marketization of our expertise in teaching and learning. So, while the appeal to professionalism remains indispensable to our efforts at going public, it also is clear that this appeal is no longer "ours." Reformers have gotten the memo to frame standardization-for-competition as "professionalization" and this professionalization as democratization.

In light of this trend, I echo Marshall's call for us to engage our publics directly on questions of reform (177). Indeed, an alternate realist style is an attempt to dramatize the distinct *quality* of professional judgment when going public. Where I diverge from Marshall, however, is in my hope for "the position and language of profession" (150) as a response to reform. The central appeal that Marshall notes, our capacity for expert judgment in context that represents our diverse publics' experiences with literacy (176), is being absorbed by the realist style of contemporary reform. In that style, the diverse contexts for literacy learning and use can *only* be addressed by a dynamic, open, and innovative marketplace of expertise. An expanded marketplace, moreover, means greater democratic access for those conventionally marginalized by the monopoly of professionalism. Granted, the consequences of this reappropriation are still uncertain, so I am not arguing that we should suspend our appeals to professionalism as the bulwark of democracy. But the capacity of reform to perform our professional style should give us pause. How *can* we appeal to the publicness of our professional judgment when that appeal is now up for grabs?

While this is not the explicit question guiding translingual inquiry, our contemporary scholarly conversations suggest a methodology suited to the challenges of going public. Like an alternate realist style, the translingual paradigm urges us to scale down: it encourages "an attitude of deliberative inquiry" (Horner, Lu, Royster, and Trimbur 2011, 304) toward language difference among our students and our publics. The purpose of this scaling down is to scale up: through teacher development (Canagarajah 2016), assessment (Dryer 2016), history (Trimbur 2016), and pedagogical theories/practices (Bawarshi 2016; Cushman 2016; Guerra 2016; Leonard and Nowacek 2016; Shipka 2016), we can not only codify professional values but also improve access to opportunity for *all* students. As Ellen Cushman (2016) argues, the shared concern of translingual inquiry is to ensure that it, as an emancipatory project, *doesn't* turn out like the others in composition (238). Cushman's concern is that while we may have critiqued our "content or place of practice" through innovations like the literacy narrative, service learning, and community engagement, we "did so without naming and altering the fundamental tenets that structure the understandings, values, and practices of first year writing courses or the genres taught therein and their important place in maintaining the social inequities that perpetuate them" (239). Specifically, we never fully acknowledged the role of our expertise in the "language and sign system hierarchies . . . implicit in, indeed necessary for, imperialism" (240). To decolonialize meaning making in composition, Cushman suggests, we must reposition our professionalism as a means of fighting the systemic inequalities our students and publics experience. In this light, translingual inquiry can help us reclaim the publicness of our expertise.

While Cushman highlights the limits of professionalism as public representation, her critique also illuminates the specifically rhetorical struggles of going public in composition. We claim that our contextual judgment is more democratically representative than standardization, but we rarely articulate our publicness *except* through the conventional appeal of professionalism, in which we need the right people to serve the right purposes. Amid the institutional and governmental K–16 reforms of the 1990s and early 2000s, the limit of this rhetorical style was concerning.[3] We could anticipate our professionalism being constrained or reduced, but ultimately, it seemed, our standing would remain intact: we would offer expert contextualism for democratic representation; reformers would offer standardization for accountability and competitiveness; and the stalemate between these educational aims would prevent any single reform from building the totalizing energy needed for transformational change. In the contemporary neoliberal context, however, our rhetorical limit points toward a more immediate concern. Certainly, we continue to claim that we alone can offer expert judgment for the public good, but we are no longer the only ones making this appeal. Contemporary reform groups also invoke equity to position themselves as agents of justice. As ETS's Doug Baldwin asked the 2015 CCCC panel, what serves the public good—an open or a closed marketplace of expertise? With this question, Baldwin went for professionalism's jugular, recognizing that we in composition defend a "sheltered labor market" (Freidson 1994, 259–60) as a necessary compensation for the risk, sunk time, and lost earnings associated with our extended educations. In the contemporary moment, however, this argument is rendered unintelligible by reform's emphasis on student cost. From reformers' perspective, the preservation of professionalism prevents students from competing in the global economy.

The power implicit in the framing of Baldwin's question illustrates our need for rhetorical innovation when going public. The pluralism of professionalism must find new ways of contending with the standardization of neoliberalism. Translingualism appears to meet this challenge by fulfilling what Keith Gilyard (2016) calls the "moral arc of composition studies" (284). It promises to join pluralism to policy. But if, as Gilyard argues, language standards are the "flip side" of language rights

(285–86), it is not clear how we might distinguish our plural-
ism-for-democracy from reform's claims of standardization-for-
competition-for-equity. What differentiates translingualism from
composition's other responses to standardization, like construc-
tivism, locality, or fairness? Why should translingualism fare any
better as a rhetoric of professionalism? Despite similar reserva-
tions about translingualism's readiness to be "put to work" (Lu
and Horner 2016, 207), however, Gilyard recognizes in translingual inquiry an opportunity to demonstrate the public good of
our judgment. We can document students' basic writing experiences (288), both for us in composition and for our publics.
And, we can circulate accounts of these experiences to serve
the function of public formation. Gilyard reads the prehistory
of basic writing at the City University of New York (CUNY) as
a sign that student organizations *can* gather around basic writing's value, and that public inquiry into these students' experiences with teaching and learning *can*—if only momentarily and
incrementally—reopen otherwise calcified debates over access,
standards, and reform. With this reading of basic writing's history, Gilyard suggests a theory and practice for going public
amid the uncertainties of contemporary reform. We may invite
our publics to authorize our professional judgment as accurate,
faithful, and just representations of public experience. Or, in
the terms of this book, we may invite antiprofessional participation for democratic inclusion.

Certainly, such antiprofessionalism is a rhetoric of professionalism: the implicit claim of translingualism is that our contextual judgment is more adequate to democratic representation
than standardization-for-competition. As a response to reform,
this appeal is conventional, and this conventionality, I believe,
is what Gilyard means by translingualism's need for "rhetorical
refinement" (289). But the potential of a rhetorically refined
translingualism is worth considering. Translingual inquiry may
help us innovate on composition's conventional style as we go
public beyond our professional boundaries. It may help us identify and dramatize acts of teaching, learning, and assessment
that disclose the values and payoffs of pluralism. And, it may

help us learn to invite public inquiry into the failure of reform's methods of responding to public experiences with writing. These are challenging efforts, but circulating students' inquiry into their experiences appears to be one way we may begin to dramatize the judgment of professionalism against the backdrop of the neoliberal scene.

WHAT MAY BE NEXT

On April 14, 2016, a three-judge panel reversed *Vergara v. California,* a court ruling that would have cut tenure and other job protections for the state's K–12 public school teachers (Blume, Resmovits, and Kohli 2016). Students Matter, the organization backing *Vergara,* claimed that union protections of ineffective teachers were blocking students' democratic access to opportunity. To ensure constitutionally adequate educations, Students Matter argued, we must implement deregulatory policy change: end "permanent employment" (tenure), revise ineffective dismissal statutes, and improve on "last in, first out" layoff policies. But the panel ruled that *Vergara* could not demonstrate how teacher protections in themselves had diminished access to opportunity, and the ruling was overturned.

Vergara's argument is familiar. Like Complete College America, Students Matter (2016) claims to expand access for underserved students. The right thing to do for equity and democracy, in this view, is to dissolve professional protections for teachers. *That way* there can be a competitive marketplace of educational expertise rather than a moribund professional monopoly. Once we remove such barriers to innovation, we can finally satisfy our national democratic errand. The *difference* between Students Matter and CCA, however, lies in the stories they tell. CCA threatens national decline caused by a failed system. Students Matter does this as well, but its appeals rest on student testimony, particularly that of fifteen- and sixteen-year-old sisters Beatriz and Elizabeth Vergara. The Vergaras claimed that their teachers had failed to provide quality instruction and that such a failure had deprived them of future opportunities. For this reason, the sisters (as guided by Students Matter) were petitioning the state to eliminate teacher protections. Not only does Students Matter advance the conventional deregulationist reform agenda, then, but it does so by republicizing reform debate. It pits the public against professionals via public participation.

Looking at *Vergara*'s tactics as a composition professional can be discouraging. Here seems to be the future of reform debate: the spokespersons for deregulation are our students, and the antiprofessionalism of public participation serves not professionalism but the cause of deregulation. Moreover, deregulation would appear to have absorbed the appeal of a translingual critique: an open marketplace of expertise ensures that educators' expertise is adequate to all students' literacy experiences. With these reversals in mind, we might look at students' potential as "public" voices and recoil from what seems like a staged spectacle of publicity. But I argue that the *Vergara* strategy points toward the need for more public voices, not fewer. Yes, *Vergara* invites public critical inquiry into the local consequences of professional judgment, and such an invitation resonates with the antiprofessionalism of the pragmatic tradition. But in its eagerness to advance the deregulatory policy positions advocated by its funder, the Broad Foundation, Students Matter reduces occasions for public participation to a series of set pieces. In Wells's (1996) term, Students Matter ventriloquizes its publics. What this conversation needs, I argue, is something we professionals can provide: a return to acts of literacy education, public inquiry into local experience, and the circulation of this inquiry. Such an approach may affirm professional standing, or this approach may point toward the need for reform. But this tactic would begin to break the professionalism-deregulation stalemate of debate and suggest an alternate role for professionals in relation to their publics. In addition to speaking for our publics, we might also attempt to circulate their inquiry as a response to venture philanthropists like the Broad Foundation. We might go public so that others may also speak for us.

Of course, K–12 teacher protections are different from composition's professionalism. But as the *New York Times* reported in April 2016, *Vergara* is going national with cases in New York and Minnesota (Rich 2016). Students Matter has seized on the appeal to justice through access and is seeking opportunities to scale up from the stories of Beatriz and Elizabeth Vergara to a deregulatory model of policy change. I find it hard *not* to imagine a case like *Vergara* turning toward us with groups like Complete College America claiming that uneven outcomes in "pre-major learning" (like first-year writing) undermine students' access to opportunity. To improve on the way undergraduate education meets the aim of equity, then, we need to open up our instruction and support systems (like writing centers) to innovation. Without this innovation, the argument is likely to go, we will have abandoned our democratic errand.

We in composition need innovation on our existing defenses of professionalism to contend with these arguments for reform. To be sure, we need bureaucracy, reframing, and public engagement as ways of attending to consequences, improving existing policies, and forming inquiry-driven publics amid reform debate. But we also need to complement these approaches for countering the appeals of reform and for inviting public participation in the discussion about who can serve the good of access. As we encounter arguments like those rehearsed in *Vergara*, we will need to perform our inquiry as a way of inviting the public naming of the tools of professionalism and markets. Then, perhaps, we can invite our publics to debate those tools and their costs. Such a debate may reward us as professionals, but perhaps not with conventional standing so much as with an opportunity for building solidarity. The democracy on offer from an alternate realist style, in other words, is not expert judgment for increasing access to opportunity. It is an opportunity for our publics to assess the publicness of judgments made on their behalf.

Is this offer wise? It is certainly not comprehensive. As I noted in chapter 3, the pragmatic question in a situation is "how long one's view should be in any given act such that any decision is based on a total evaluation of the consequences of one's actions within a larger but bounded environment" (Crick 2010, 77). In taking up a long view on publicness, I am seeking to avoid claims of serving our students, for today this appeal can authorize a neoliberal marketplace of service providers and elevate consumer choice to the role of making public policy. In pragmatic terms, that is my political-economic tough-mindedness about the world and what is possible within it. Rather, I am attempting to create opportunities for students to reassess claims made on their behalf. That is my tender-mindedness about publics and what is possible via publicity.

Is this "the discourse of student need" (Horner 2015) once again? I don't believe it is. This is not saying that our students need us; rather, it is saying that I believe students will find contemporary reforms inadequate as a response to their experiences with writing. That's a fine line, and I can see how an appeal to student experience sounds very much like need as the warrant for professional standing. Here, perhaps, is where all efforts at going public eventually fall back into idealist style. But in the process of performing our inquiry to invite public participation, circulating accounts of this inquiry, and responding to the formation of potential counterpublics, we will have envisioned and enacted a more public professionalism. This shift would begin to engage the possibilities of Dewey's participatory vision. These are the possibilities that animate this book. But to assess these possibilities more fully, we will need new inquiries into this book's proposals, for we can be sure that the appeals of reform will continue to evolve and we will need to innovate further for the next rounds of change.

NOTES

1. "A Theory of Ethics for Writing Assessment: Risk and Reward for Civil Rights, Program Assessment, and Large-Scale Testing," chaired by Ellen Cushman. (Poe et al. 2015)

2. Although DeLuca and Peeples's stance differs from Linda Adler-Kassner's, both see opportunity for critics to engage publics through discussions arising from corporately controlled messaging. In *The Activist WPA*, for example, Adler-Kassner (2008) describes how the NCTE responded to the College Board's 2005 introduction of an SAT writing exam (74–80). By engaging in the national reform jeremiad, Adler-Kassner argues, writing professionals were able to change stories about writing and writers. Although I doubt Adler-Kassner would characterize

reframing the reform jeremiad as "critique through spectacle" (DeLuca and Peeples 2002, 133–34), her approach recognizes the quality of discourse on the public screens of reform. It is spectacular, and it calls for a similarly spectacular response.

3.   This period saw the K–12 national standards discussion in the early 1990s, the higher education reform discussions following the 1995 Boyer Report, and the standards and accountability discussions following No Child Left Behind in the early 2000s and the Spellings Commission in the mid-2000s.

REFERENCES

Achieve, Inc. 2004. "Ready or Not: Creating a High School Diploma That Counts I Achieve." *American Diploma Project.* http://www.achieve.org/pub lications/ready-or-not-creating-high-school-diploma-counts.

Achieve, Inc., and the National Governors Association. 2005. "An Action Agenda for Improving America's High Schools." *National Education Summit on High Schools: Achieve Inc. and National Governors Association.* https://www.nga.org/Files/pdf/0502actionagenda.pdf.

Adler-Kassner, Linda. 2008. *Activist WPA: The Changing Stories about Writing and Writers.* Logan: Utah State University Press.

Adler-Kassner, Linda, and Susanmarie Harrington. 2002. *Basic Writing as a Political Act: Public Conversations about Writing and Literacies.* Cresskill: Hampton Press.

Adler-Kassner, Linda, and Susanmarie Harrington. 2010. "Responsibility and Composition's Future in the Twenty-First Century: Reframing 'Accountability.'" *College Composition and Communication* 62 (1): 73–99.

Adler-Kassner, Linda, and Peggy O'Neill. 2010. *Reframing Writing Assessment to Improve Teaching and Learning.* Logan: Utah State University Press.

Anson, Chris M., Scott Filkins, Troy Hicks, Peggy O'Neill, Kathryn Mitchell Pierce, and Maisha Winn. 2013. "NCTE Position Statement on Machine Scoring." *NCTE Position Statement on Machine Scoring.* http://www.ncte.org/pos itions/statements/machine_scoring.

Anson, Chris M., and L. Lee Forsberg. 1990. "Moving Beyond the Academic Community Transitional Stages in Professional Writing." *Written Communication* 7 (2): 200–231. https://doi.org/10.1177/0741088390007002 002.

Arum, Richard, and Josipa Roksa. 2011. *Academically Adrift: Limited Learning on College Campuses.* Chicago: University of Chicago Press.

Asen, Robert. 2009a. *Invoking the Invisible Hand: Social Security and the Privatization Debates.* East Lansing: Michigan State University Press.

Asen, Robert. 2009b. "Ideology, Materiality, and Counterpublicity: William E. Simon and the Rise of a Conservative Counterintelligentsia." *Quarterly Journal of Speech* 95 (3): 263–288. https://doi.org/10.1080/00335630903140630.

Asen, Robert, and Daniel C. Brouwer. 2001. *Counterpublics and the State.* Albany, NY: SUNY Press.

Association of American Colleges and Universities. 2014. "VALUE Rubric Development Project." *Association of American Colleges and Universities.* June 23. https://www.aacu.org/value/rubrics.

Astin, Alexander W. 2011. "'Academically Adrift': A Closer Look at the Numbers." *The Chronicle of Higher Education,* February 14, sec. Commentary. http://www.chronicle.com/article/Academically-Adrift-a/126371/.

Aune, James Arnt. 2002. *Selling the Free Market: The Rhetoric of Economic Correctness.* New York: Guilford Press.

DOI: 10.7330/9781607326540.c006

Banta, Trudy W., and Gary R. Pike. 2007. "Revisiting the Blind Alley of Value Added." *Assessment Update* 19 (1): 1–2, 14–15. https://doi.org/10.1002/au .191.

Bawarshi, Anis. 2016. "'Beyond the Genre Fixation: A Translingual Perspective on Genre." *College English* 78 (3): 243–49.

Benjamin, Roger, Marc Chun, and Chris Jackson. 2009. "The Collegiate Learning Assessment's Place in the New Assessment and Accountability Space." http://cae.org/images/uploads/pdf/04_The_Collegiate_Learning_Assess ments_Place_in_the_New.pdf.

Blakesley, David. 1999. "Kenneth Burke's Pragmatism—Old and New." In *Kenneth Burke and the 21st Century*, ed. Bernard L. Brock, 71–98. Albany: State University of New York Press.

Blume, Howard, Joy Resmovits, and Sonali Kohli. 2016. "In a Win for Unions, Appeals Court Reverses Ruling That Threw out Teacher Tenure in California." *Latimes.com*, April 14. http://www.latimes.com/local/lanow/la-me-ln -court-rejects-bid-to-end-teacher-tenure-in-california-marking-huge-win-for -unions-20160414-story.html.

Bomer, Randy, Bill Bass, MaryCarmen Cruz, Doug Hesse, Henry Kiernan, Jennifer Ochoa, Diane Waff, Kylene Beers, and Kent Williamson. 2009. "A Report of the NCTE Review Team on the July 2009 Draft of the Common Core English Language Arts State Standards." National Council of Teachers of English. http://citeseerx.ist.psu.edu/viewdoc/download?doi=10.1.1.569 .3135&rep=rep1&type=pdf.

Bousquet, Marc. 2003. "Composition as Management Science." In *Tenured Bosses and Disposable Teachers: Writing Instruction in the Managed University*, ed. Marc Bousquet, Tony Scott, and Leo Parascondola, 11–35. Carbondale: Southern Illinois University Press.

Burke, Kenneth. 1969a. *A Grammar of Motives*. Berkeley: University of California Press.

Burke, Kenneth. 1969b. *A Rhetoric of Motives*. Berkeley: University of California Press.

Burke, Kenneth. 1972. *Dramatism and Development*. Barre. Clark University Press.

Burke, Kenneth. 1984a. *Attitudes toward History*. Berkeley: University of California Press.

Burke, Kenneth. 1984b. *Permanence and Change: An Anatomy of Purpose*. Berkeley: University of California Press.

Burns, Alexander. 2017. "Legal Challenges Mount Against Trump's Travel Ban." *The New York Times*, January 30, 2017. https://www.nytimes.com/2017/01/30 /us/legal-challenges-mount-against-trumps-travel-ban.html.

Calhoon-Dillahunt, Carolyn. 2012. "'Important Focus, Limited Perspective.' Review of *Academically Adrift* by Richard Arum and Josipa Roksa." *College Composition and Communication* 63 (3): 495–99.

Cambridge University Institute for Manufacturing. 2015. "JIT: Just in Time Manufacturing." Accessed July 31, 2015. http://www.ifm.eng.cam.ac.uk/research /dstools/jit-just-in-time-manufacturing/.

Canagarajah, Suresh. 2016. "Translingual Writing and Teacher Development in Composition." *College English* 78 (3): 265–73.

Chaput, Catherine. 2010. "Rhetorical Circulation in Late Capitalism: Neoliberalism and the Overdetermination of Affective Energy." *Philosophy & Rhetoric* 43 (1): 1–25.

Charbonneau, David. 2012. "Directed Learning Activities–'Just in Time' for the Basic Skills Writer | Another Word." *Another Word: From the Writing Center at the University of Wisconsin–Madison*, March 12. http://writing.wisc.edu/blog /?p=2030.

Common Core State Standards. 2008. "Benchmarking for Success: Ensuring US Students Receive a World-Class Education." http://www.corestandards.org /assets/0812BENCHMARKING.pdf.

Common Core State Standards Initiative. 2015. "Standards in Your State." http://www.corestandards.org/standards-in-your-state/.

Complete College America. 2011. "Time Is the Enemy." http://completecol lege.org/docs/Time_Is_the_Enemy.pdf.

Complete College America. 2012. "Remediation: Higher Education's Bridge to Nowhere." http://www.completecollege.org/docs/CCA-Remediation-final.pdf.

Complete College America. 2013. "The Game Changers: Are States Implementing the Best Reforms to Get More College Graduates?" http://www.completecol lege.org/pdfs/CCA%20Nat%20Report%20Oct18-FINAL-singles.pdf.

Concerned Student 1950. 2015. "List of Demands from Concerned Student 1-9-5-0 Group." *Columbia Daily Tribune*, October 23, 2015. http://www.columbia tribune.com/list-of-demands-from-concerned-student-group/pdf_345ad844 -9f05-5479-9b64-e4b362b4e155.html.

Council for Aid to Education. 2016. "CLA+ Collegiate Learning Assessment: Measuring Critical Thinking for Higher Education." Accessed January 31, 2016. http://cae.org/flagship-assessments-cla-cwra/cla/about-cla/.

Crick, Nathan. 2010. *Democracy and Rhetoric: John Dewey on the Arts of Becoming*. Columbia: University of South Carolina Press.

Cushman, Ellen. 1999. "The Public Intellectual, Service Learning, and Activist Research." *College English* 61 (3): 328–336. https://doi.org/10.2307/379072.

Cushman, Ellen. 2003. "Beyond Specialization: The Public Intellectual, Outreach, and Rhetoric Education." In *The Realms of Rhetoric: The Prospects for Rhetoric Education*, ed. Joseph Petraglia and Deepika Bahri, 171–85. Albany: State University of New York Press.

Cushman, Ellen. 2016. "Translingual and Decolonial Approaches to Meaning Making." *College English* 78 (3): 234–42.

Danisch, Robert. 2007. *Pragmatism, Democracy, and the Necessity of Rhetoric*. Columbia: University of South Carolina Press.

DeLuca, Kevin Michael. 1999. *Image Politics: The New Rhetoric of Environmental Activism*. New York: Guilford Press.

DeLuca, Kevin Michael, and Jennifer Peeples. 2002. "From Public Sphere to Public Screen: Democracy, Activism, and The 'Violence' of Seattle." *Critical Studies in Media Communication* 19 (2): 125–151. https://doi.org/10.1080 /07393180216559.

DeVos, Betsy. 2017. "Opening Statement of Betsy DeVos, Nominee for US Secretary of Education, US Senate Committee on Health, Education, Labor and Pensions." January 17, 2017. https://www.help.senate.gov/imo/media/doc /DeVos.pdf.

Dewey, John. 1927. *The Public and Its Problems*. Athens: Swallow/Ohio University Press.

Dewey, John. 1935. *Art as Experience*. New York: Minton, Balch and Company.

Dewey, John. 1969. "The Moral Struggle or the Realizing of Ideals." In *The Early Works of John Dewey*, vol. 3: *1882–1898*, ed. Jo Ann Boydston, 372–81. Carbondale: Southern Illinois University Press.

Dryer, Dylan B. 2016. "Appraising Translingualism." *College English* 78 (3): 274–83.

Durst, Russel K. 1999. *Collision Course: Conflict, Negotiation, and Learning in College Composition*. Urbana: National Council of Teachers of English.

Dzur, Albert W. 2008. *Democratic Professionalism: Citizen Participation and the Reconstruction of Professional Ethics, Identity, and Practice*. University Park: The Pennsylvania State University Press.

Edbauer, Jenny. 2005. "Unframing Models of Public Distribution: From Rhetorical Situation to Rhetorical Ecologies." *Rhetoric Society Quarterly* 35 (4): 5–24. https://doi.org/10.1080/02773940509391320.

Ericsson, Patricia Freitag. 2006. "The Meaning of Meaning: Is a Paragraph More than an Equation?" In *Machine Scoring of Student Essays: Truth and Consequences*, ed. Patricia Freitag Ericsson and Richard H. Haswell, 28–37. Logan: Utah State University Press.

Ericsson, Patricia Freitag, and Richard H. Haswell, eds. 2006. *Machine Scoring of Student Essays: Truth and Consequences*. Logan: Utah State University Press.

Farmer, Frank. 2013. *After the Public Turn: Composition, Counterpublics, and the Citizen Bricoleur*. Logan: Utah State University Press.

Festenstein, Matthew. 1997. *Pragmatism and Political Theory: From Dewey to Rorty*. Chicago: University of Chicago Press.

Fish, Stanley. 1998. "Truth and Toilets: Pragmatism and the Practices of Life." In *The Revival of Pragmatism: New Essays on Social Thought, Law, and Culture*, ed. Morris Dickstein, 418–33. Durham, NC: Duke University Press.

Fleckenstein, Kristie S. 2008. "A Matter of Perspective: Cartesian Perspectivalism and the Testing of English Studies." *JAC* 28 (1/2): 85–121.

Fleischer, Cathy. 2000. *Teachers Organizing for Change: Making Literacy Learning Everybody's Business*. Urbana, IL: National Council of Teachers of English.

Flower, Linda. 2008. *Community Literacy and the Rhetoric of Public Engagement*. Carbondale: Southern Illinois University Press.

Fox, Tom. 1999. *Defending Access: A Critique of Standards in Higher Education*. Portsmouth, NH: Boynton/Cook.

Freidson, Eliot. 1994. *Professionalism Reborn*. London: Blackwell.

Freidson, Eliot. 2001. *Professionalism: The Third Logic*. Chicago: University of Chicago Press.

Gallagher, Chris W. 2005. "We Compositionists: Toward Engaged Professionalism." *JAC* 25 (1): 75–99.

Gallagher, Chris W. 2007. *Reclaiming Assessment: A Better Alternative to the Accountability Agenda*. Portsmouth, NH: Heinemann.

Gallagher, Chris W. 2010. "At the Precipice of Speech: English Studies, Science, and Policy (Ir)relevancy." *College English* 73 (1): 73–90.

Gallagher, Chris W. 2011. "Being There: (Re)Making the Assessment Scene." *College Composition and Communication* 62 (3): 450–76.

Gallagher, Chris W. 2012. "The Trouble with Outcomes: Pragmatic Inquiry and Educational Aims." *College English* 75 (1): 42–60.

Gardner, Traci. 2010. "Stories Make It Personal." *NCTE Inbox Blog*, March 2. http://ncteinbox.blogspot.com/2010/03/stories-make-it-personal.html.

Gere, Anne Ruggles. 1991. "Public Opinion and Teaching Writing." In *The Politics of Writing Instruction: Postsecondary*, ed. Richard H. Bullock, John Trimbur, and Charles I. Schuster, 263–76. Portsmouth, NH: Boynton/Cook.

Gilyard, Keith. 2016. "The Rhetoric of Translingualism." *College English* 78 (3): 284–89.

Goldblatt, Eli. 2005. "Alinsky's Reveille: A Community-Organizing Model for Neighborhood-Based Literacy Projects." *College English* 67 (3): 274–295. https://doi.org/10.2307/30044637.

Goldblatt, Eli. 2007. *Because We Live Here: Sponsoring Literacy beyond the College Curriculum*. Cresskill: Hampton Press.

Grabill, Jeffrey T. 2007. *Writing Community Change: Designing Technologies for Citizen Action*. Cresskill, NJ: Hampton Press.

Grabill, Jeffrey T. 2012. "Community-Based Research and the Importance of a Research Stance." In *Writing Studies Research in Practice: Methods and Methodologies*, ed. Lee Nickoson and Mary P. Sheridan, 210–19. Carbondale: Southern Illinois University Press.

Graff, Gerald, and Cathy Birkenstein. 2008. "A Progressive Case for Educational Standardization." *Academe* 94 (3): 16–20.

Graves, Donald H. 1985. "All Children Can Write." *Learning Disabilities Focus* 1 (1): 36–43.

Guerra, Juan C. 2016. "Cultivating a Rhetorical Sensibility in the Translingual Writing Classroom." *College English* 78 (3): 228–33.

Gunn, Giles. 1988. *The Culture of Criticism and the Criticism of Culture*. New York: Oxford University Press.

Gunner, Jeanne. 2012. "'Everything That Rises . . .' Review of *Academically Adrift* by Richard Arum and Josipa Roksa." *College Composition and Communication* 63 (3): 491–95.

Hansen, Kristine. 2012. "The 'Framework for Success in Postsecondary Writing': Better than the Competition, Still Not All We Need." *College English* 74 (6): 540–43.

Hariman, Robert. 1989. "The Rhetoric of Inquiry and the Professional Scholar." In *Rhetoric in the Human Sciences*, ed. Herbert W. Simons, 211–32. Newbury Park: Sage Publications.

Hariman, Robert. 1995. *Political Style: The Artistry of Power*. Chicago: University of Chicago Press. https://doi.org/10.7208/chicago/9780226316284.001.0001.

Harris, Elizabeth A., and Ford Fessenden. 2015. "'Opt Out' Becomes Anti-Test Rallying Cry in New York State." *The New York Times*, May 20. http://www.nytimes.com/2015/05/21/nyregion/opt-out-movement-against-common-core-testing-grows-in-new-york-state.html.

Harris, Joseph. 2012. *A Teaching Subject: Composition since 1966*. Logan: Utah State University Press.

Harris, Joseph. 1997. "Review: Reclaiming the Public Sphere." *College English* 59 (3): 324–331. https://doi.org/10.2307/378383.

Haswell, Richard H. 2006. "Automatons and Automated Scoring: Drudges, Black Boxes, and Dei Ex Machina." In *Machine Scoring of Student Essays: Truth and Consequences*, ed. Patricia Freitag Ericsson and Richard H. Haswell, 57–78. Logan: Utah State University Press.

Haswell, Richard H. 2012. "'Methodologically Adrift.' Review of *Academically Adrift* by Richard Arum and Josipa Roksa." *College Composition and Communication* 63 (3): 487–91.

Hauser, Gerard A. 2014. "Afterword: The Possibilities for Dewey Amidst the Angst of Paradigm Change." In *Trained Capacities: John Dewey, Rhetoric, and Democratic Practice*, ed. Brian Jackson and Gregory Clark, 233–48. Columbia: University of South Carolina Press.

Headden, Susan. 2011. "How the Other Half Tests." *Washington Monthly*, October. https://washingtonmonthly.com/magazine/septoct-2011/how-the-other -half-tests-2/.

Herrington, Anne, and Charles Moran. 2001. "What Happens When Machines Read Our Students' Writing?" *College English* 63 (4): 480–499. https://doi.org /10.2307/378891.

Herrington, Anne, and Charles Moran. 2006. "WritePlacer Plus in Place: An Exploratory Case Study." In *Machine Scoring of Student Essays: Truth and Consequences*, ed. Patricia Freitag Ericsson and Richard H Haswell, 114–29. Logan: Utah State University Press.

Hess, Amanda. 2017. "How a Fractious Women's Movement Came to Lead the Left." *The New York Times*, February 7, 2017. https://www.nytimes.com/2017/02/07 /magazine/how-a-fractious-womens-movement-came-to-lead-the-left.html.

Higgins, Lorraine D., and Lisa D. Brush. 2006. "Personal Experience Narrative and Public Debate: Writing the Wrongs of Welfare." *College Composition and Communication* 57 (4): 694–729.

Hirschman, Albert O. 1970. *Exit, Voice, and Loyalty: Responses to Decline in Firms, Organizations, and States*. Cambridge, MA: Harvard University Press.

Hirschman, Albert O. 1991. *The Rhetoric of Reaction: Perversity, Futility, Jeopardy*. Cambridge, MA: Belknap/Harvard University Press.

Horner, Bruce. 2000. "Traditions and Professionalization: Reconceiving Work in Composition." *College Composition and Communication* 51 (3): 366–398. https://doi.org/10.2307/358741.

Horner, Bruce. 2015. "Rewriting Composition: Moving beyond a Discourse of Need." *College English* 77 (5): 450–79.

Horner, Bruce, and Min-Zhan Lu. 1999. *Representing The "Other": Basic Writers and the Teaching of Basic Writing*. Urbana, IL: National Council of Teachers of English.

Horner, Bruce, Min-Zhan Lu, Jacqueline Jones Royster, and John Trimbur. 2011. "Language Difference in Writing: Toward a Translingual Approach." *College English* 73 (3): 303–21.

Hull, Glynda. 2001. "Hearing Other Voices: A Critical Assessment of Popular Views on Literacy and Work." In *Literacy: A Critical Sourcebook*, ed. Ellen Cushman, Eugene R. Kintgen, Barry M. Kroll, and Mike Rose, 660–84. Boston: Bedford/St. Martin's.

Human Readers. 2015. "Professionals against Machine Scoring of Student Essays in High-Stakes Assessment." http://humanreaders.org/petition/.

Jackson, Brian, and Scott R. Stroud. 2014. "John Dewey, Kenneth Burke, and the Role of Orientation in Rhetoric." In *Trained Capacities: John Dewey, Rhetoric, and Democratic Practice*, ed. Brian Jackson and Gregory Clark, 47–64. Columbia: University of South Carolina Press.

James, William. 1907. *Pragmatism, a New Name for Some Old Ways of Thinking; Popular Lectures on Philosophy*. New York: Longmans, Green, and Co. https://doi .org/10.1037/10851-000.

Jones, Edmund. 2006. "Accuplacer's Essay-Scoring Technology: When Reliability Does Not Equal Validity." In *Machine Scoring of Student Essays: Truth and Consequences*, ed. Patricia Freitag Ericsson and Richard H. Haswell, 93–113. Logan: Utah State University Press.

Kestenbaum, Victor. 2002. *The Grace and the Severity of the Ideal: John Dewey and the Transcendent*. Chicago: University of Chicago Press.

Klein, Stephen, Roger Benjamin, Richard Shavelson, and Roger Bolus. 2007. "The Collegiate Learning Assessment: Facts and Fantasies." *Evaluation Review* 31 (5): 415–439. https://doi.org/10.1177/0193841X07303318.

Koopman, Colin. 2009. *Pragmatism as Transition: Historicity and Hope in James, Dewey, and Rorty*. New York: Columbia University Press.

Krugman, Paul. 2015. "The Expansionary Austerity Zombie." *The New York Times: The Conscience of a Liberal*, November 20. http://krugman.blogs.nytimes.com /2015/11/20/the-expansionary-austerity-zombie/.

Kuh, George D. 2007. "Risky Business: Promises and Pitfalls of Institutional Transparency." *Change: The Magazine of Higher Learning*, January 1. https://doi .org/10.3200/CHNG.39.5.30-37.

Larson, Magali Sarfatti. 1977. *The Rise of Professionalism: A Sociological Analysis*. Berkeley: University of California Press.

Leonard, Rebecca Lorimer, and Rebecca Nowacek. 2016. "Transfer and Translingualism." *College English* 78 (3): 258–64.

Long, Elenore. 2008. *Community Literacy and the Rhetoric of Local Publics*. West Lafayette, IN: Parlor Press.

Lu, Min-Zhan. 1992. "Conflict and Struggle: The Enemies or Preconditions of Basic Writing?" *College English* 54 (8): 887–913. https://doi.org/10.2307/378444.

Lu, Min-Zhan, and Bruce Horner. 2016. "Introduction: Translingual Work." *College English* 78 (3): 207–18.

MacKinnon, Jamie. 1998. "Becoming a Rhetor: Developing Writing Ability in a Mature, Writing-Intensive Organization." In *Writing in the Workplace: New Research Perspectives*, ed. Rachel Spilka, 41–55. Carbondale: Southern Illinois University Press.

Marshall, Margaret J. 1995. *Contesting Cultural Rhetorics: Public Discourse and Education, 1890–1900*. Ann Arbor: University of Michigan Press. https://doi.org /10.3998/mpub.13953.

Marshall, Margaret J. 2004. *Response to Reform: Composition and the Professionalization of Teaching*. Carbondale: Southern Illinois University Press.

Matter, Students. 2016. http://studentsmatter.org.

Mayher, John S. 1990. *Uncommon Sense: Theoretical Practice in Language Education*. Portsmouth, NH: Boynton/Cook.

Mayher, John S. 1999. "Reflections of Standards and Standard Setting: An Insider/Outsider Perspective on the NCTE/IRA Standards." *English Education* 31 (2): 106–21.

Mayher, John S. 2010. "Visions of the Future." In *Reading the Past, Writing the Future: A Century of American Literacy Education and the National Council of Teachers of English*, ed. Erika Lindemann, 395–422. Urbana, IL: National Council of Teachers of English.

McComiskey, Bruce. 2012. "Bridging the Divide: The (Puzzling) 'Framework' and the Transition from K–12 to College Writing Instruction." *College English* 74 (6): 537–40.

McGee, Tim. 2006. "Taking a Spin on the Intelligent Essay Assessor." In *Machine Scoring of Student Essays: Truth and Consequences*, edited by Patricia Freitag Ericsson and Richard H. Haswell, 79–92. Logan: Utah State University Press.

Miller, Carolyn R. 2010. "Should We Name the Tools?: Concealing and Revealing the Art of Rhetoric." In *The Public Work of Rhetoric: Citizen-Scholars and Civic Engagement*, ed. John Ackerman and David Coogan, 19–38. Columbia: University of South Carolina Press.

Miller, Richard E. 1998a. *As If Learning Mattered: Reforming Higher Education.* Ithaca, NY: Cornell University Press.

Miller, Richard E. 1998b. "The Arts of Complicity: Pragmatism and the Culture of Schooling." *College English* 61 (1): 10–28. https://doi.org/10.2307/379055.

Mortensen, Peter. 1998. "Going Public." *College Composition and Communication* 50 (2): 182–205. https://doi.org/10.2307/358513.

Muyumba, Walton. 2014. "'All Safety Is an Illusion': John Dewey, James Baldwin, and the Democratic Practice of Public Critique." In *Trained Capacities: John Dewey, Rhetoric, and Democratic Practice*, ed. Brian Jackson and Gregory Clark, 159–73. Columbia: University of South Carolina Press.

Myers, Miles. 1994. "NCTE's Role in Standards Projects." *English Education* 26 (1): 67–76.

NSHE (Nevada System of Higher Education). 2010. "Complete College Nevada: Increasing the Number of Nevadans with Certificates and Degrees by 2020." https://www.unr.edu/Documents/provost/provosts-office/ccaNSHE.pdf.

O'Neill, Peggy, Linda Adler-Kassner, Cathy Fleischer, and Anne-Marie Hall. 2012. "Creating the 'Framework for Success in Postsecondary Writing.'" *College English* 74 (6): 520–24.

Office of the Provost (University of Nevada, Reno). 2017. "Complete College America." Accessed February 3, 2017. https://www.unr.edu/provost/complete-college-america.

Parks, Steve, and Eli Goldblatt. 2000. "Writing Beyond the Curriculum: Fostering New Collaborations in Literacy." *College English* 62 (5): 584–606. https://doi.org/10.2307/378963.

Perelman, Les. 2014. "Flunk the Robo-Graders." *BostonGlobe.com*, April 30. https://www.bostonglobe.com/opinion/2014/04/30/standardized-test-robo-graders-flunk/xYxc4fJPzDr42wlK6HETpO/story.html.

Perelman, Les. 2015. "Our Stand Against the Robo-Graders" September 27.

Poe, Mya, Norbert Elliot, Bob Broad, and David Slomp. 2015. "A Theory of Ethics for Writing Assessment: Risk and Reward for Civil Rights, Program

Assessment, and Large-Scale Testing." Panel presented at the Conference on College Composition and Communication: Risk and Reward, Tampa, FL.

Poe, Mya, Norbert Elliot, John Aloysius Cogan, and Tito G. Nurudeen. 2014. "The Legal and the Local: Using Disparate Impact Analysis to Understand the Consequences of Writing Assessment." *College Composition and Communication* 65 (4): 588–611.

Porter, James E., Patricia Sullivan, Stuart Blythe, Jeffrey T. Grabill, and Libby Miles. 2000. "Institutional Critique: A Rhetorical Methodology for Change." *College Composition and Communication* 51 (4): 610–642. https://doi.org/10.2307/358914.

Prelli, Lawrence J., Floyd D. Anderson, and Matthew T. Althouse. 2011. "Kenneth Burke on Recalcitrance." *Rhetoric Society Quarterly* 41 (2): 97–124. https://doi.org/10.1080/02773945.2011.553768.

Putnam, Ruth Anna. 1998. "The Moral Impulse." In *The Revival of Pragmatism: New Essays on Social Thought, Law, and Culture*, ed. Morris Dickstein, 62–71. Durham, NC: Duke University Press. https://doi.org/10.1215/9780822382522-005.

Redd, Teresa. 2012. "'An HBCU Perspective on Academically Adrift.' Review of *Academically Adrift* by Richard Arum and Josipa Roksa." *College Composition and Communication* 63 (3): 499–506.

Rhoades, Gary. 1998. *Managed Professionals: Unionized Faculty and Restructuring Academic Labor*. Albany: State University of New York Press.

Rhoades, Gary. 2007. "The Study of the Academic Profession." In *Sociology of Higher Education: Contributions and Their Contexts*, ed. Patricia J. Gumport, 113–46. Baltimore: Johns Hopkins University Press.

Rich, Motoko. 2016. "Teacher Tenure Is Challenged Again in a Minnesota Lawsuit." *The New York Times*, April 13. http://www.nytimes.com/2016/04/14/us/teacher-tenure-is-challenged-again-in-a-minnesota-lawsuit.html.

Richardson, Seth A. 2017. "Having Trouble Trying to Call Dean Heller? So Is Everyone Else." *Reno Gazette-Journal*. February 2, 2017. http://www.rgj.com/story/news/politics/2017/02/02/having-trouble-trying-call-dean-heller-so-everyone-else/97422474/.

Rose, Mike. 1985. "The Language of Exclusion: Writing Instruction at the University." *College English* 47 (4): 341–359. https://doi.org/10.2307/376957.

Rose, Mike. 1988. "Narrowing the Mind and Page: Remedial Writers and Cognitive Reductionism." *College Composition and Communication* 39 (3): 267–302. https://doi.org/10.2307/357468.

Rose, Mike. 1995. *Possible Lives: The Promise of Public Education in America*. Boston: Houghton Mifflin.

Rose, Mike. 2009. *Why School?: Reclaiming Education for All of Us*. New York: New Press.

Rose, Mike. 2010. "Writing for the Public." *College English* 72 (3): 284–92.

Roskelly, Hephzibah, and Kate Ronald. 1998. *Reason to Believe: Romanticism, Pragmatism, and the Teaching of Writing*. Albany: State University of New York Press.

Saultz, Andrew, and Michael P. Evans. 2015. "The Opt-Out Movement Is Gaining Momentum—Education Week." *Education Week*, June 10. http://www.edweek.org/ew/articles/2015/06/10/the-opt-out-movement-is-gaining-momentum.html.

Shipka, Jody. 2016. "Transmodality in/and Processes of Making: Changing Dispositions and Practice." *College English* 78 (3): 250–57.

Soliday, Mary. 2002. *The Politics of Remediation: Institutional and Student Needs in Higher Education.* Pittsburgh: University of Pittsburgh Press.

Spellmeyer, Kurt. 1993. *Common Ground: Dialogue, Understanding, and the Teaching of Composition.* Englewood Cliffs: Prentice Hall.

Stob, Paul. 2005. "Kenneth Burke, John Dewey, and the Pursuit of the Public." *Philosophy & Rhetoric* 38 (3): 226–247. https://doi.org/10.1353/par.2005.0022.

Stob, Paul. 2016. "Thomas Davidson's Pragmatist Rhetorical Style—or, Rhetorical Pragmatism without Philosophical Pragmatism." Conference Presentation presented at the Rhetoric Society of America Biennial Conference, Atlanta, GA, May.

Strauss, Valerie. 2016. "The Testing Opt-out Movement Is Growing, despite Government Efforts to Kill It." *Washington Post,* January 31, sec. Answer Sheet. https://www.washingtonpost.com/news/answer-sheet/wp/2016/01/31/the-testing-opt-out-movement-is-growing-despite-government-efforts-to-kill-it/.

Strickland, Donna. 2011. *The Managerial Unconscious in the History of Composition Studies.* Carbondale: Southern Illinois University Press.

Stroud, Scott R. 2006. "Pragmatism and Orientation." *Journal of Speculative Philosophy* 20 (4): 287–307.

Stroud, Scott R. 2010. "What Does Pragmatic Meliorism Mean for Rhetoric?" *Western Journal of Communication* 74 (1): 43–60. https://doi.org/10.1080/10570310903463737.

Stroud, Scott R. 2011. "John Dewey and the Question of Artful Criticism." *Philosophy & Rhetoric* 44 (1): 27–51. https://doi.org/10.5325/philrhet.44.1.0027.

Suhor, Charles. 1994. "National Standards in English: What Are They? Where Does NCTE Stand?" *English Journal* 83 (7): 25–27. https://doi.org/10.2307/820544.

Summerfield, Judith, and Philip M. Anderson. 2012. "A Framework Adrift." *College English* 74 (6): 544–47.

The Council of Writing Program Administrators, The National Council of Teachers of English, and The National Writing Project. 2012. "Framework for Success in Postsecondary Writing." *College English* 74 (6): 525–33.

Trimbur, John. 1991. "Literacy and the Discourse of Crisis." In *The Politics of Writing Instruction: Postsecondary,* ed. John Trimbur and Richard H. Bullock, 277–95. Portsmouth, NH: Heinemann.

Trimbur, John. 2011. "Articulation Theory and the Problem of Determination: A Reading of Lives on the Boundary." In *Solidarity or Service: Composition and the Problem of Expertise,* ed. John Trimbur, 14–31. Portsmouth, NH: Heinemann.

Trimbur, John. 2016. "Translingualism and Close Reading." *College English* 78 (3): 219–27.

Varnum, Robin. 1986. "From Crisis to Crisis: The Evolution toward Higher Standards of Literacy in the United States." *Rhetoric Society Quarterly* 16 (3): 145–165. https://doi.org/10.1080/02773948609390746.

"Voluntary System of Accountability (VSA) Administration and Reporting Guidelines: AAC&U VALUE Rubrics—Demonstration Project." 2012. American Association of Colleges and Universities. https://cp-files.s3.amazonaws

.com/32/AAC_U_VALUE_Rubrics_Administration_Guidelines_20121210 .pdf.

Wan, Amy J. 2011. "In the Name of Citizenship: The Writing Classroom and the Promise of Citizenship." *College English* 74 (1): 28–49.

Webber, Jim, and Maja Wilson. 2012. "Do Grades Tell Parents What They Want and Need to Know?" *Phi Delta Kappan* 94 (1): 30–35. https://doi.org /10.1177/003172171209400106.

Webber, Jim, and Maja Wilson. 2013. "Moving Beyond 'Parents Just Want to Know the Grade!'" In *De-Testing and de-Grading Schools: Authentic Alternatives to Accountability and Standardization,* edited by Joe Bower and P. L Thomas, 210–18. New York: Peter Lang.

Weiser, M. Elizabeth. 2008. *Burke, War, Words: Rhetoricizing Dramatism.* Columbia: University of South Carolina Press.

Wells, Susan. 1996. "Rogue Cops and Health Care: What Do We Want from Public Writing?" *College Composition and Communication* 47 (3): 325–341. https:// doi.org/10.2307/358292.

West, Cornel. 1989. *The American Evasion of Philosophy: A Genealogy of Pragmatism.* Madison: University of Wisconsin Press. https://doi.org/10.1007/978-1-349 -20415-1.

White, Edward M. 1991. "Use It or Lose It: Power and the WPA." *WPA. Writing Program Administration* 15:3–12.

White, Edward M. 2010. "English Professor as Public Figure: My Days in Court." *College English* 73 (2): 183–95.

Wilson, Maja. 2006. "Apologies to Sandra Cisneros." *Rethinking Schools* 20 (3): 42–46.

"WriteLab." 2016. *WriteLab.* http://home.writelab.com/.

ABOUT THE AUTHOR

JIM WEBBER is an assistant professor of English at the University of Nevada, Reno.

INDEX

Academically Adrift, 87–88, 126, 129.
   See also Arum, Richard; Roksa,
   Josipa
access: as advanced by translingualism, 155–57; as central term and
   value of composition professionals, 31, 112–13, 141, 154; as
   central term and value of reform,
   11–14, 106; as represented by
   appeals to "citizenship," 61–65;
   as a rhetoric for disciplining
   professionals, 53; as served by
   professional reappropriation of
   standardizing reforms, 45, 47, 49,
   54, 60, 123; as served by standardizing reforms, 21, 65–67, 158–60;
   as undermined by machine
   scoring, 101, 120–22. *See also*
   education reform; neoliberalism;
   professionalism; standardization;
   translingualism; Wan, Amy J.
Accuplacer Software, 98
Adler-Kassner, Linda: on pragmatic
   judgment in composition studies, 3; on reframing as pragmatic
   response to reform, 13, 15, 25,
   72, 81–84; on reframing as redirecting reform, 39, 72, 76, 78; on
   reframing in neoliberal context,
   110, 112; reframing in relation
   to pragmatic tradition, 91–95;
   on reframing in relation to the
   American Association of Colleges and Universities (AAC&U),
   125; in relation to image events,
   161–62n2; on representing basic
   writers' experiences, 12, 122; on
   telling stories as "going public,"
   119. *See also* Harrington, Susanmarie; O'Neill, Peggy; reframing;
   West, Cornel
Althouse, Matthew T., 139–40(n2)
American Association of Colleges

and Universities (AAC&U): in
   neoliberal reform context, 125,
   150; as response to standardizing reforms, 18–19, 42(n3), 44,
   103. *See also* Collegiate Learning
   Assessment (CLA); reframing;
   Voluntary System of Accountability (VSA)
American Diploma Project, 18,
   42(n4)
Anderson, Floyd J., 139–40(n2)
Anderson, Philip, 19, 86–87
Anson, Chris M., 19, 28, 130–32
antiprofessionalism: as an alternate
   rhetoric of professionalism, 157–
   61; as enacted through professional critique, 90–91; gendered
   consequences of, 154; as inviting
   public authorization of professional judgment, 8, 23, 34, 63,
   112–16, 139–47; as professional
   commitment to public usefulness,
   150; as professional sponsorship
   of counterpublic resistance, 20,
   22, 100–105; as quality of pragmatic tradition, 6; as response to
   neoliberal reform scene, 68; rhetorical style of, 40. *See also* Burke,
   Kenneth; Dewey, John; "going
   public"; public engagement;
   translingualism; West, Cornel
Arum, Richard, 87–88, 129
Asen, Robert, 28, 42–43(n7)
assessment. *See* disparate impact
   analysis; education reform;
   "going public"; machine scoring;
   standardization
Aune, James Arnt, 28

Baldwin, Doug, 142–44, 156
"being there." *See* Gallagher, Chris W.
Birkenstein, Cathy: in composition's conversations about "going